THE QUEST
OF THE
HOLY GRAIL

THE QUEST
OF THE
HOLY GRAIL

Jessie L. Weston

DOVER PUBLICATIONS, INC.
Mineola, New York

Copyright

Copyright © 2001 by Dover Publications, Inc.
All rights reserved under Pan American and International Copyright Conventions.

Published in Canada by General Publishing Company, Ltd., 30 Lesmill Road, Don Mills, Toronto, Ontario.

Bibliographical Note

This Dover edition, first published in 2001, is an unabridged republication of a standard edition of the work originally published in 1913 by G. Bell & Sons Ltd., London.

Library of Congress Cataloging-in-Publication Data

Weston, Jessie Laidlay, 1850–1928.
    The quest of the Holy Grail / Jessie L. Weston.
       p. cm.
    Originally published: London : G. Bell, 1913.
    Includes bibliographical references and index.
    ISBN 0-486-41977-0 (pbk.)
    1. Grail—Romances—History and criticism. 2. Arthurian romances—History and criticism. 3. Civilization, Medieval, in literature. 4. Knights and knighthood in literature. 5. Quests (Expeditions) in literature. I. Title.

PN686.G7 W7 2001
809'.915—dc21

                          2001028454

Manufactured in the United States of America
Dover Publications, Inc., 31 East 2nd Street, Mineola, N.Y. 11501

PREFACE

In the following pages I have endeavoured to give, as clearly and concisely as possible, a description of the literature composing the Grail cycle, an analysis of its content, and a survey of the leading theories to which this perplexing body of romance has given rise.

Lacking as we do MS. evidence for the initial stages in the development of the story, ignorant of the precise time and place of its birth as a theme for popular romance, it is impossible to present a theory that shall have behind it the weight and authority of established fact. There will always be too many missing links, however skilfully the chain be woven. But the theory set forth in these pages is that which, after twenty years spent in close and constant study of the subject, I believe to be the only one capable of meeting all the varied conditions of the problem. It is not as yet complete, and in the absence of fresh discoveries in the field of MS. literature perhaps may never be entirely so, but the fact that it places the question on a new and wider basis, freeing it from the limits of mere literary criticism, introduces a new element of encouragement. If the study of the Grail Quest fall, as I hold it does, within the field of Comparative Religion, we can call to our aid scholars whose interest lies otherwise outside the fascinating, but to some minds perhaps superficial, realm of romantic literature.

The whole problem gains in depth and importance, it passes alike from those problems which are the province of the scholar versed in philology and the establishment of critical texts, and from those which are the chosen playground of the enthusiastic amateur ; and that will in itself be clear gain, for if the Grail problem has suffered from the arid literalism of the former, it has suffered even more from the fantastic speculations of the latter.

The ' Secret of the Grail ' I hold to be above all a ' human ' problem, a subject of profound human interest, and one which touches such deep springs of human thought and need that it requires to be handled by those whose interest lies in dealing with the workings of the soul, as much as with the expression of literary intelligence.

The real difficulty of the question lies in the fact that it is at once literary, religious, and popular—this latter inasmuch as it deals with the transmission from one age to another, of a certain distinct and characteristic body of practice and belief. Its complete and harmonious solution demands the active and sympathetic co-operation of minds too apt to stand aloof from one another, too apt to view each other's work with distrust, or even contempt. There is need here for the trained accuracy of the critic of incomplete, and often corrupt, texts; of the zeal and industry of the collector and transcriber of popular beliefs; above all, of the aid of the scholar whose highest aim and keenest interest lie in ascertaining what men have believed, and how, in their journey through the ages, they have conceived and expressed their relation to the Unseen. When these Seekers after Truth will consent to work together in harmony, doing full justice each to the other's view, then, and not till then, the ' Secret of the Grail ' will cease to be a secret.

If the Grail Quest were the offspring of mere literary imagination, however poetic and picturesque, if its literature were merely a romantic cycle which in this twentieth century possessed nothing but an archaic interest, it would have no place in this Quest Series. It is precisely upon the view set forth in these pages as to its origin and development, that it can base a claim to admission among themes of vital and enduring interest. In the short space at my disposal it has been impossible to give evidence and authorities for all the statements made, but readers may rest assured that there is nothing stated as fact in these pages for which there is not ample evidence, no hypothesis which is not based upon sound and probable premises. Others may interpret the evidence somewhat differently, but it exists, and its importance and extent will, I think, be a matter of surprise to many readers. Among those readers there may be some who, more at home than myself in those mysterious regions where pre-Christian touched with Christian belief, may be able to throw light on the most obscure passages through which the fascinating legend passed on its way to complete Christian Mystic evolution.

JESSIE L. WESTON.

PARIS, *June* 1913.

CONTENTS

CHAPTER I

THE end of the twelfth and the beginning of the thirteenth centuries, a period covering, at its utmost extent, not more than some fifty years, witnessed the formation of a body of romantic literature, verse and prose, dealing with the quest for, and attainment of, a mysterious Talisman, varying in provenance, form, and effect, though known always by the same name.

Thus, while that Talisman is always known as the Grail, the term may connote a mysterious and undescribed Food-providing Object, which comes and goes without visible agency; a Stone, endowed with food- and life-giving properties, which also from time to time assumes the *rôle* of an oracle; a 'Holy' Object, the form of which is not indicated, wrought of gold and precious stones, and emitting a brilliant light; a Reliquary; the Dish from which our Lord and His Disciples ate the Paschal Lamb at the Last Supper, or the Cup of that Meal; the Vessel (sometimes that just mentioned, whether Cup or Dish, sometimes one specially made for the purpose) in which Joseph of Arimathea received the Blood which flowed from the Wounds of the Redeemer; finally, a mysterious combination of these two latter forms with the Chalice of the Eucharist. Even in this final, highly ecclesiastized shape the Grail retains traces of its earlier origin, appearing and disappearing automatically and mysteriously, and, as one romance definitely states, being of no material substance whatsoever, " for of wood was it not, nor of any kind of metal nor of stone was it wrought, neither of horn, nor of bone."

And as the Grail itself varies, so do also the results arising from a successful fulfilment of the Quest. At first the object is the cure of the Guardian of the Talisman, an enigmatic personage, generally known as the Fisher, or Maimed, King, who is helpless from the effects either of a wound, of extreme old age, or of illness caused by the failure of the Quester, and with the cure of the ruler the restoration of fertility to his land, which lies waste while the Quest is unfulfilled. In the final form the result of the Quest is rather the

attainment of spiritual enlightenment by
the Quester, who, beholding the deep things
of God, passes at the moment of vision from
the world—" and thenne sodenly his soule
departed to Jhesu Christ, and a grete multi-
tude of Angels bare his soule up to heven."

And if the content of the literature be
thus varied and perplexing, not less so are
the external form and fortunes.

As indicated above, the Grail texts, as
preserved to us, are restricted both in number
and period. We have no text which, in its
present form, can be dated earlier than the
last quarter of the twelfth century, or later
than the first quarter of the thirteenth, but,
whereas the material used by the verse-
writers of the cycle is undoubtedly derived
from earlier and no longer existing versions
of the theme, and the story itself is therefore
older than any form we now possess, so that
the *terminus a quo* cannot be definitely fixed,
the *terminus ad quem* is certain.

After the early years of the thirteenth century no Grail romance was composed; for some
reason or other the theme which had been so
potent a source of inspiration had suddenly
and completely lost its power. And yet it
had not lost its interest for the reader; for we
have fourteenth and fifteenth-century MSS.,
alike of the poems and prose romances, and
both were among the earliest subjects of the
printer's art. In fact, that particular version

of the Grail Quest which owed its inception
to the popularity of the *Lancelot* story, and
now forms an integral portion of that lengthy
romance, from whence it was taken over in
an enlarged form into the *Tristan*, was
reprinted over and over again (there are
eight or nine editions of the *Lancelot* and at
least six of the *Tristan*, not to mention the
Spanish and Portuguese translations, which
account for three or four more editions apiece);
while the English translation, in Malory's
noble prose, remains a classic to this day.

Thus, in discussing the Grail literature, the
student finds himself at the very outset confronted with not one, but a group of problems.
What are we to understand by ' The Grail ' ?
What is the real origin of the story ?   What
was the cause of the initial popularity of this
theme ?   What the cause of its sudden disappearance from the field of literature ?
Should or should not the Quest of the Holy
Grail be reckoned among those spiritual
' Quest ' problems with which it is the object
of this series to deal ?   In the following
pages we will endeavour, so far as the incomplete character of the evidence at our
disposal will permit, to suggest a satisfactory
answer to these questions.

CHAPTER II

THE earliest version of the Grail story we possess, in point of MS. date, is the *Perceval*, or *Conte du Graal*, of Chrétien de Troyes, the most famous of Northern French poets of the twelfth century. Sixteen MSS. of the work have been preserved to us, but, with the possible exception of a portion of the ' Riccardiana ' text, none are earlier than the first half of the thirteenth century.

A writer of great facility and considerable literary charm, Chrétien was the author of a group of narrative poems dealing with the heroes of Arthurian romantic tradition— poems distinguished rather by fluency and finish (a modern German critic has remarked that Chrétien, like a conjuror, " could shake perfectly turned couplets out of his sleeves ") than by poetical imagination, and depth of thought. *Perceval,* his last poem, is not, from the literary point of view, his best work ; that distinction belongs rather to the *Chevalier au Lion,* or *Yvain,* a poem of which German, Icelandic, and English translations

5

exist, and which bears a close affinity to the Welsh Mabinogi of *The Lady of the Fountain.* It is to the subject-matter, rather than to the style, that the *Perceval* owes its fame. The direct source, for the poem is no invention, has not yet been discovered. Chrétien states that he found the tale in a book given to him by Philip, Count of Flanders, to whom the work is dedicated. Left unfinished by the author, the poem, already fairly long, over 10,000 lines, received subsequent additions from the hand of three independent writers —Wauchier de Denain, otherwise known as a translator of certain *Lives of the Saints*; Manessier, who wrote at the command of the Countess Jeanne of Flanders (in whose service Wauchier, from evidence lately discovered, also appears to have been); and Gerbert, who is undoubtedly to be identified with Gerbert de Montreuil, a well-known poet of the first quarter of the thirteenth century. The section due to Gerbert is inserted between the continuations of Wauchier and Manessier, and is only preserved in two MSS. The whole length of the poem now extends to over 60,000 lines.

To students of the Grail literature the *Perceval* presents a most fascinating problem, or rather, group of problems : the real nature of Chrétien's source is unknown ; while the later writers are ostensibly completing his poem not one of the three shows the smallest

care to adhere to Chrétien's version, each
betrays his knowledge of other, and widely
differing, forms of the story ; so that the result
of the work as a whole is in the highest
degree perplexing and contradictory.

Especially is this the case with the first
continuator, Wauchier, who, as is now very
generally recognized, is drawing for his
authority upon texts anterior to Chrétien.
He not only knows a version of the *Perceval*
story differing widely from that utilized by
his predecessor, but he knows another, and
older, Grail Quester, in the person of Gawain.
Drawing on the version of a certain Bleheris,
who, he tells us, was born and bred in Wales,
he relates a story of Gawain's adventures at
the Grail Castle so picturesque in form, so
vivid in narration, that, in spite of its brevity,
it ranks as one of the best of mediæval
chivalric tales.   And if the *Perceval* gives us
more than one Grail hero it also varies in its
account of the Grail ; Chrétien, in mysterious
fashion, tells us :

> *De fin or esmerée estoit*
> *piéres pressieuses avoit*
> *el Graal de maintes manieres—*

that it gives a light that outshines that of
the tapers, and is a holy thing, ' *tante sainte
cose est li Graaus.*'   But what it is, Cup, Dish,
or Reliquary, and why ' holy,' he never says,
nor does he explain the relation, if any,

existing between the Grail and the Bleeding
Lance which forms a part of the same procession.

Wauchier, in his Gawain section, knows
the Grail as ' rich,' not ' holy,' a mysterious, automatic, food-providing object, which
comes and goes at will, and serves the guests
at the feast in an unexplained and awe-
inspiring manner :

> *Le riche Graal qui servoit*
> *si que nus ne le sostenoit—*
>
> .   .   .   .   .   .
>
> *Mesire Gauvain l'esgarda*
> *trop durement se merveilla*
> *de ce qu'il servoit ensi,*
> *car ore est la, et ore est chi,*
> *a trop grant merveille li tient*
> *qu'il va si tost et revient.*
>
> (The rich Grail which served
> so that 'twas upheld by none—
>
> .   .   .   .   .   .
>
> Mesire Gawain gazed upon it,
> and very greatly he marvelled
> that it served in this fashion,
> for now 'twas there, and now 'twas here,
> and he held it for too great a marvel
> that it passed so swiftly and came again.)

This ' rich ' food-providing Grail is here
quite other than the Cup which Gawain sees
later in the great hall of the Castle, into
which a stream of blood flows ceaselessly
from the point of a Lance fixed upright
within it. This Lance is subsequently ex-

plained as being the weapon with which
Longinus pierced the side of the Saviour
as He hung on the Cross, and in a passage
interpolated in some of the later MSS. the
Grail of the feast is said to be the vessel
made by Joseph of Arimathea to receive the
Blood which flowed from the Sacred Wounds :

Voirs est que Joseph le fist fere.

('Tis true that Joseph caused it to be made.)

But this is obviously an addition, as the
point of the whole story lies in Gawain's
failure to learn what the Grail may be.

It is noticeable that Wauchier also insists
elsewhere on the mystery concerning the
Grail, and the danger of speaking of it save at
a fitting time, and in a fitting place :

S'en puet avoir et paine el mal
cil qui s'entremet a conter
fors ensi com il doit aler—

(He may have great pain and ill
who undertakes to tell of it
otherwise than it should go—)

a warning which in slightly varying forms is
more than once repeated. In yet another
passage Wauchier tells us none can speak of
the mysteries of the Grail without trembling
and changing colour. It is evident that this
poet is drawing upon sources which regard
the Grail as something ' uncanny ' and even
dangerous, rather than as a ' holy ' object;

the term ' taboo ' best expresses the idea of
the talisman derived from this section of the
Perceval.

To Manessier the Grail is quite simply
that of the ' Wauchier ' interpolation; it is
the Vessel of Joseph of Arimathea, without
any perplexing feature attached to it.

Gerbert, whose contribution is manifestly
derived from widely differing sources, con-
tents himself in the first part, which he
dignifies by the term ' *le vraie histoire*,' with
the assertion that the Grail is ' *chose saint-
isme*,' a ' most holy thing,' and in the latter
adopts the ' Joseph ' origin.

When we add that a fragmentary text,
found in two instances prefixed to Chrétien's
poem, and bearing the curious title of
Élucidation, speaks of a sevenfold quest of
the Grail, the mysteries of which, according
to ' Master Blihis,' none may reveal, and
gives a brief summary of the visit to the Fisher
King's court in terms closely agreeing with
the Bleheris-Gawain visit, it will be realized
that in this one text of the *Perceval* as now
preserved to us, we have practically a com-
pendium of the main problems besetting the
inquiry.

Of almost equal importance for critical
purposes is the *Parzival* of Wolfram von
Eschenbach, the famous Bavarian Minne-
singer. The poem, written in the opening
years of the thirteenth century, probably be-

tween 1205–16, deals with the same subject-
matter, and for much of its content covers the
same ground as that of Chrétien. It is, and
probably unless further MS. evidence should
be discovered, always will be, impossible
definitely to determine the relationship between the two works; Wolfram himself distinctly states that his source was the work
of a certain Kiot, ' the Provençal,' and
blames Chrétien for having mis-told the tale ;
at the same time the fact that no work by a
poet of the name exists, and that the parallel
sections of the French and German poems
show a close correspondence, have caused the
admirers of the French poet to assert that
Kiot is a purely fictitious personage, and that,
beyond Chrétien's poem, Wolfram had no
source save his own imagination.

While fully admitting the resemblance
between the two works, the variants, to a
critical student, are such that they can with
difficulty be ascribed to a German imagination. The whole work has manifestly been
most carefully planned with the initial aim
of exalting the fame of the house of Anjou ;
there is a long and elaborate introduction,
filling two of the sixteen books, dealing with
the adventures of Parzival's father, Gah-
muret, an Angevin prince, which betrays an
undoubted familiarity with the history and
traditions of that house ; the Grail, which is
here no Vessel but a Stone, possessing food-

bestowing and life-sustaining properties, is under the guardianship of an Order of knightly celibates, Templeisen, elected by the Grail itself, as children, their names appearing upon the Stone, which, in the same way, indicates the chosen wife of the king, who alone is allowed to marry.   If any land shall be torn with dissension for lack of a ruler, and the folk of that land pray to Heaven for aid, the Grail oracle will show the name of a knight who shall be sent forth ' as king to that kingless land.'   The introduction of this detail, which paves the way for the subsequent connection of the Swan-Knight theme with the Grail legend, is an interesting indication of the care with which the poem has been planned.   After the winning of the Grail by Parzival, his half-brother, son of his father by a Saracen princess, weds the Grail-bearer, and their son is Prester John ! Of Parzival's twin sons the elder, Kardeiss, inherits Anjou, the younger, Lohengrin, the Grail kingdom; the latter is the hero of the Swan-Knight tale in its most popular form.

Of none of these curious developments is there the least hint to be found in Chrétien's poem, and the Angevin connection, at least, hardly seems likely to have suggested itself naturally to an untravelled Bavarian knight such as we know Wolfram von Eschenbach to have been, especially at a moment when the fortunes of the house in question were dis-

tinctly on the wane. The solution of the
main problem is probably to be found in the
acceptance of Wolfram's statement as to his
source, and the view that Kiot's poem was an
amplified version of that handed to Chrétien
by Count Philip, the French and German
poems thus being independent versions of a
common original; but other problems, notably
that of the Grail itself, and its Order of
Guardian Knights, are not easily to be solved.

As a piece of constructive literature the
Parzival ranks higher than any other work
of the cycle; the whole lengthy story has
been, as suggested above, well thought out,
and the connecting thread between the various sections continuously borne in mind.
Whereas in Chrétien's much shorter version
the ostensible hero, Perceval, disappears from
sight during the recital of Gawain's adventures, and reappears in an arbitrary manner
to vanish from the scene as suddenly as he
came, the German poem, even when relating
the same sequence of incident, always keeps
him more or less in view; when Gawain
is occupying the foreground of the stage
Parzival hovers in the background, or passes
across the scene, and we have contant allusions to his actions—wherever Gawain goes
Parzival has passed before him, or follows in
his steps. The ethical motive, the development of the hero's character, ' *a brave man,
yet slowly wise*,' is well worked out, and though

the style is less finished than that of Chrétien or of Wolfram's German contemporaries, there are passages of extraordinary poetical beauty. In fact, the respective merits and characteristics of the French and German poets afford an interesting parallel to the relation between Tennyson and Browning. The one has the advantages of style, finish, and command of language, with a certain amount of insight into the workings of the mind—Chrétien's self-communing passages are very curious and ingenious; the other possesses great depth and richness of thought, a real insight into the human soul and its relation with the Unseen, and much power of poetical imagery, wedded to an extremely abrupt and obscure literary style. The *Parzival* is undoubtedly a work of genius, and one that will well repay study; it has been edited and translated with a frequency that is in itself a testimony to its literary worth and enduring interest.

As compared with these two remarkable poems the prose versions of the Grail Quest seem to the student somewhat banal and uninteresting. The earliest, and from many points of view the most important, is that by Robert de Borron, a writer whose identity has not yet been determined. It here forms the concluding portion of a trilogy, *Joseph of Arimathea*, *Merlin*, and *Perceval*, the first section of which is also preserved in a verse form. It would probably be more correct to speak of this group as a tetralogy, for the last part of the *Perceval*, subsequent to the achievement of the Quest, is devoted to the conquests and death of Arthur, which, in the original version, must have been treated at considerable length, and should of right be separately classed as a *Mort Artus*. Here we find the Christian character of the Grail fully developed; it is the Dish from which Our Lord and His Disciples ate at the Last Supper, which, given to Joseph by Pilate, was used by him to receive the Blood which flowed from the Sacred Wounds, and, being brought to Joseph by Our Lord Himself in the prison to which the Jews had consigned him, miraculously sustained him during a captivity of forty years.

Brought to Britain by Joseph, the Grail acts as an oracle, distinguishing between the good and the evil; elects its own guardian; and foretells the future course of events. At Joseph's death the Grail is committed to the charge of his brother-in-law, Brons, and shall eventually pass to the care of his grandson, son of Alain. Thus there are to be three Grail Keepers.

There are also three Tables : the Table of the Last Supper, the Grail Table, and the Round Table at Arthur's court, with its Perilous Seat, corresponding to the seat of Judas at the original table.

Here, then, while we find the Christian character of the talisman fully emphasized, and a mysterious threefold symbolism insisted upon, the whole story is closely connected with Arthur's court, through the agency of Merlin, whose story forms the second stage of Borron's trilogy. It is Merlin who constructs the Round Table after the model of its two predecessors; Merlin who reveals to the knights of Arthur's court the presence of the Grail in Britain and the necessity for the Quest; how it is preserved in the house of Brons, the Fisher King, who languishes in extreme old age, awaiting the arrival of his grandson Perceval, who, by asking concerning the Grail, shall restore him to health and youth, and become Guardian in his stead. When Perceval arrives at Arthur's court, and in company with other knights sets forth on the Heaven-announced Quest, Merlin watches over him, and, after one abortive visit, directs him finally on the road to his goal. In Borron's trilogy we have all the material for the later cyclic development of the theme. It is of course obvious that we are here in the presence of certain glaring inconsistencies; Borron is possessed with the idea that his theme is to be worked out on the basis of a mystic threefold development, but to bring this about, while at the same time he unites the story closely with Arthurian pseudo-historic

tradition, he is forced to set all probability
at defiance by prolonging the age of the
second Grail Keeper, Brons, beyond all natural
limits, spanning by this one life the gulf
between the very beginning of the Christian
era and the days of Arthur—upwards of
five hundred years !

And he in no way attempts to evade this
point; on the contrary, in the better of the
only two existing MSS., the Modena text, he
makes Brons relate to his grandson, after his
cure, the whole story of his life : how he had
seen our Lord as a Child, ' *comment il
L'avoit vëu petit Enfant,*' which would seem to
indicate that he himself had been born before
the beginning of the Christian era ! At the
same time we never have any indication that
the life of Perceval's father, even when considered as Brons' son, exceeded the ordinary
limit of human life; as a rule he dies in the
flower of manhood. There can, I think, be
very little doubt that the attraction of the
Arthurian tradition has operated disastrously
upon Borron's original scheme of a Grail
romance, and that the form which he ultimately gave to his work was quite other than
that originally planned.

Borron's work was probably composed in
the closing years of the twelfth century, and
it certainly formed the starting-point and
model for the development of the combined
Grail and Arthur themes as a formidable

body of cyclic romance. A very distinct
note of difference between the poetical and
prose versions is the comparative unim-
portance of the Arthurian element in the
former ; Perceval certainly seeks Arthur's
court with the hope of obtaining knighthood,
but, once launched on his adventures, he
makes only brief and occasional returns
thither. His Grail Quest is quite unconnected
with Arthur, or the Round Table. Similarly,
although Gawain is an Arthurian knight,
' *vom häuse aus*,' at home there, and nowhere
else, his Grail Quest is a purely independent
and personal experience, unshared by any
other knight.

It is quite otherwise in the prose romances :
here the Quest of the Grail is announced at
Arthur's court ; it is no chance adventure
befalling one individual knight, but a formal
undertaking in which all participate under
certain fixed rules of time and procedure—a
courtly quest is for a year and a day, the
knights must ride separately, or in pairs, and
on their return make public recital of their
adventures—and the fulfilment is closely
connected with the ability to fill uninjured a
vacant seat at the Round Table, fraught with
direst peril to whomsoever shall wrongfully
occupy it.

But there is another element connected
with the development of the Arthurian cyclic
Quest which, as yet hardly recognized, bids

fair, as the result of recent research, to become an important factor in our critical investigation of the literature—that is, the growing importance of the *Lancelot* story.

To those who only know Arthurian romance through the medium of two English writers, Malory and Tennyson, it will doubtless be a surprise to learn that the knight whose fame in the later stages of the cyclic development practically overshadowed that of all others, was but a late-comer into the charmed circle. Chrétien's *Perceval* knows him not ; the *Parzival* makes but casual allusion to one special adventure ; in neither poem is Lancelot a member of the gorgeous court surrounding the British king. The circumstances under which Lancelot first sprang into popularity do not affect our present inquiry, but it seems quite certain that his story developed at first outside the Arthurian cycle proper, and on parallel lines—*i.e.* while Borron provided the historic Arthur tradition with a Grail Quest in which Lancelot played no part, an unknown writer added to the romantic tale of the love of Lancelot for Arthur's queen a Quest in which Lancelot shared with Gawain and Perceval the honour of search and sight, though not of achievement.

This romance, which is generally known as the *Perlesvaus* from the peculiar form given to the hero's name, was for a long time a *crux* to the Arthurian critic ; we did not know where to place it. On the one hand, it showed obvious traces of influence by versions akin both to Chrétien and Wolfram; on the other, it as obviously knew nothing of the final *Galahad* form of the story. The late Mr. Alfred Nutt was so impressed by the evidences of borrowing on the part of the author, or compiler, that, in his *Studies in the Legend of the Holy Grail*, he omitted the text altogether from his classification and abstract of romances; it was, he held, too unoriginal to be of use. On the other hand, Dr. Sebastian Evans, in a fine translation of the romance, published in the Temple Classics under the title of *The High History of The Holy Grail*, claimed for it the honour of being "the original story of Sir Perceval and the Holy Grail, whole and incorrupt as it left the hands of its first author."

As in most cases of exaggerated estimates, the truth lies midway between these two extremes. Recent research has drawn attention to the fact that certain of the existing *Lancelot* MSS. refer to that romance as forming a part of the 'Story of Perceval and the Grail,' which "is head and end of all the other stories." Other texts retain the *Perlesvaus* form of the name, and refer to adventures found only in that romance, while the concluding passage of the *Perlesvaus* announces the beginning of the war against Claudas for the recovery of Lancelot's patri-

mony. If we also note that the *Perlesvaus*
records the death of Guenevere, it becomes
clear that this romance cannot have formed
part of a cycle concluding in the orthodox
manner with the death of Arthur as a consequence of the treachery of wife and nephew ;
the story must rather have formed part of a
parallel group devoted to the fortunes of the
dispossessed hero, Lancelot, and concluding
with his return to his own land, the death of
his royal ' *amie* ' having severed the link
which bound him to Arthur's court. This
theory gains additional probability when we
note the fact that the *Merlin* section of the
ordinary cycle is paralleled by an abridged
version of the life and adventures of that
mysterious personage, inserted, *tant bien
que mal*, in the earlier portion of the
Lancelot, while the *Mort Artus* proper has
been drawn upon for the account of Arthur's
defeat of Frollo and conquest of Gaul, here
combined with the expedition against King
Claudas. Also the *Lanzelet* of Ulrich von
Zatzikhoven, a poem which is recognized as
representing an early form of the story, concludes in the manner suggested above—*i.e.*
with the reconquest of, and return of the hero
to, his own hereditary kingdom.

We can thus, with comparative certainty, fix
the position to be assigned to the *Perlesvaus*
in its present form, but its source as a Grail
romance, and relation to other texts of the

same family, are less easily to be determined.
The Grail here is the Vessel in which Joseph
of Arimathea collected the Sacred Blood, and
the Lance, the weapon of Longinus, but in
actual fact the talismans correspond to those
which, in the Gawain story, are differentiated
from the Grail proper—*i.e.* we have here
again a Lance bleeding into a Cup.

Nor does the hero achieve the original
Quest, for although, by force of arms, he
eventually gains possession of the Grail
Kingdom, the Fisher King is already dead, as
a result of the illness caused by the deferred
question.   There seems reason to believe that
we have here the working over, not for the
first time, of a romance which, in its original
verse form, was an early rendering of the
Christianized theme.

Christian and mystical to a high degree the
Perlesvaus is, imbued with a fierce spirit of
militant proselytism; the pagan opponents
of the hero are, when overcome, confronted
with the ruthless alternative of conversion
or death; the unbaptized adherents of the
Old Law can hope for no mercy at the hands
of this exponent of forcible Christianity,
whose career is marked by hecatombs of
slaughtered pagans !   The whole tone is most
curiously different from that of the *Parzival*,
where the Saracens, knights and ladies alike,
are endowed with all chivalric virtues and
courtly graces; their conversion to Chris-

tianity only places the final seal on their manifold excellences.

The *Perlesvaus* should, then, be considered as a *Lancelot* Quest, contemporary, in its present prose form, with the *Perceval* of Robert de Borron. But when the *Lancelot* romance became finally, and definitely, incorporated with the Arthurian pseudo-historic cycle, a change in the Quest section was necessary. Lancelot had become far too popular and imposing a figure for his share in the great Quest to be any longer a subordinate and abortive one ; at the same time, his relations with Guenevere, which were the *fons et origo* of his connection with the cycle, had been developed in a manner which could not be ignored and must be retained. Yet these very relations forbade him to become the hero of a Quest which the gradual process of literary evolution had endowed with a strongly spiritual and ethical character. There was only one solution of the difficulty : Lancelot must be provided with a son, by another than Guenevere, who, equipped with all the qualifications, spiritual and chivalric, necessary for a Grail hero, should achieve the Quest, and pass away in the achievement, leaving his father undisturbed in his position as premier Knight of the court, with an added halo of glory as father of the Grail-winner. That this is the real object of the Galahad *Queste* is no longer disputed; as it stands now it forms an excrescence on the cycle, adding nothing of necessity to its content, and, were it taken away, injuring in nowise its coherence. The Quest interlude over, Lancelot and Guenevere fall back into their previous relations, and the story progresses to its traditional and inevitable end.

Thus, on the lines and with the object above defined, the Galahad *Quête du Saint Graal*, the final romance of the cycle, was constructed, and this is the form in which the story, through the medium of Malory's abridged translation of the cycle, and the poems founded by Tennyson on that trans-lation, is best known to English readers, though, of late years, the fame of Wagner's great music-drama, *Parsifal*, based largely upon the poem of von Eschenbach, has made them aware of the fact that other versions of the Grail story do, in fact, exist.

The Galahad *Queste* differs from the other Grail texts in being practically an inde-pendent form of the story, unrelated to any preceding version; the only romance with which it is really organically connected is the *Lancelot*. The fact that a new hero had to be invented—for Galahad, it must be emphasized, exists for, and in, the *Quête du Saint Graal* only, and plays no part in any other romance—left the author free to arrange for him a series of adventures unhampered

by any previously existing tradition.   Here
and there faint echoes of earlier themes are
heard : Galahad comes to a Castle of Maidens
—so did Perceval, but under widely differing
circumstances ; Galahad visits a mysterious
cemetery—so do other Arthurian heroes, but
with other object and other result ; the king
at whose court the Grail is wont to show
itself is still the Fisher King, but his land is
no longer ' waste ' and the ' maiming ' has
been transferred to two other personalities.
Perceval figures in the story ; but he is no
longer the impetuous unrestrained lad whose
strongly marked individuality has impressed
a curious stamp of reality on the earlier
romances, but a correct and blameless knight,
as colourless as Galahad himself.   Traces of
his earlier story may still be found in his
possession of a recluse aunt, and a sister
whose character for devotion and sanctity
is on a par with that of the immaculate hero ;
and some MSS. even retain allusions to the
loss of his father's heritage, but very little
trace of the earlier *Perceval* Quest remains.

And the earliest Grail hero, Gawain, fares
still worse. If Perceval has been ' improved '
out of knowledge, Gawain has been debased
beyond recognition; the knight *sans peur*
and *sans reproche* of our old English tradition,
of earlier cyclic fame, has become a hardened
reprobate, immoral, reckless, irreverent, inferior not only to Galahad and Perceval

but to the knights of later invention, and of Lancelot's family, Bors and Hector. Throughout the whole romance Gawain is held up as the ' awful example,' everything a good knight ought not to be !

In spite of some fine passages, such as that describing Lancelot's experiences at Corbenic, the romance, as a whole, is a lamentable declension from the first poetical versions of the story. Numerous texts, both MS. and printed editions, of the *Queste* exist, but none show variants other than those due to more or less careful copying, and the impression left by the work is that of a ' *Tendenz-Schrift*,' a story invented at a special time, for a special purpose, and in no way dependent upon an earlier form.

In the final stage of the evolution of the Arthurian cycle, when its tentacles, stretching far and wide, had laid hold of the originally quite independent *Tristan* theme, and drawn it within the meshes of the Arthurian net, the Galahad Quest became enlarged in order to permit of the participation, not only of Tristan himself, but also of other knights who had become more or less closely connected with him. Thus, in the interminable MSS. (such as Bibl. Nat. Fonds Français, 112) which represent the final stages of Arthurian romance, we have an enlarged form of the *Queste*, drawn out to wearisome length by the interpolation of banal adventures. In this

final form the story passed the frontiers of
France, and has been preserved in Spanish and
Portuguese translations. Italy apparently
knew it earlier, for while the *Tavola Ritonda*
gives the later *Tristan* form, the *Chantari di
Lancilotto* and a prose text, which had the
curious fate of being translated from Italian
into Hebrew, and is preserved in a MS. of
the Vatican, follows the ordinary *Mort Artus*
form.

Standing in the same relation to the
Galahad Quest as Borron's *Joseph of Arimathea* does to his *Perceval*, is the romance
known as the *Grand Saint Graal*; this is
simply the *Joseph* expanded by the insertion
of numerous adventures relating the fortunes
of Joseph's son, Josephes, and his conversion mission, which eventually leads him to
Britain.· The various heathen kings converted by him play more or less important
parts in the story; the genealogy of the
Grail Guardians, the descent of Lancelot
and Galahad from the chosen family, all
are carefully worked out, and the whole
wrought into a superficial harmony alike
with the prose *Lancelot* and the *Quête du
Saint Graal*. The work is in all probability
by the same hand as the last-named romance,
and it is distinctly the most wearisome and
least characteristic member of the entire
cycle.

The texts above enumerated form a more

or less interrelated body of literature, and show a gradual and progressive evolution from a chivalric romance, endowed with a certain element of mysterious adventure, to a purely religious, and in its final stage highly ecclesiasticized, treatise of edification. There still remains, however, one Grail text, which lies outside the general line of evolution, and, though comparatively late in date, is based upon elements contemporaneous with the earliest stages of the story.

This is *Diu Crône*, by Heinrich von dem Tûrlin, a German writer of the first quarter of the thirteenth century. It is a long, rambling poem, devoted to the praise of Gawain, and containing a mass of tradition relating to that hero, parts of which are, undoubtedly, of very early origin. Here Gawain not merely seeks, but attains, the Grail, thereby releasing the Grail King from a spell which imposes upon him, though dead, the semblance of life—a curious consummation, met with nowhere else. Here the Grail is a Reliquary, containing a Host, with which the king is nourished, while he also partakes of the Blood which drops from the Lance, again a unique feature. *Diu Crône* has, so far, not been the subject of a careful and detailed study, and an opinion as to its true position in the cycle and real critical value cannot safely be given. The material with which it deals belongs, obviously, to an early stage of the Arthurian tradition, and it is quite possible that the work may ultimately furnish us with valuable links in the chain of evidence.

The texts preserved to us may, then, be classed either according to their form, verse or prose, or according to the personality of the hero. In the first case we have two, in the second, three groups.

Of verse forms we have the *Perceval* of Chrétien de Troyes, and his continuators, which includes of course the Bleheris-*Gawain* version; the *Parzival* of Wolfram von Eschenbach; *Diu Crône* of Heinrich von dem Tûrlin; and the verse form of Borron's *Joseph*, preserved in a unique MS.

The prose texts are Robert de Borron's trilogy, of which *Perceval* represents the Quest section; *Perlesvaus*; and the *Quête du Saint Graal*, with its introduction, the *Grand Saint Graal*.

Classed according to the hero, we have three groups: Gawain, in the Bleheris text, preserved by Wauchier de Denain and *Diu Crône*; Perceval, in the poem of Chrétien with its three continuations, the *Parzival* of von Eschenbach, the *Perceval* of Borron, and the *Perlesvaus*; Galahad, in the *Queste*, and in that romance only.

The discrepancy in the number of texts assigned to each hero points to the conclusion that, while the *Gawain* form marks the first appearance of the story as a popular tale, before it has become a recognized literary theme, and therefore belongs rather to the category of folk-tale than to that of romantic literature, and the *Galahad* marks the stage of final development, when the vitality of the theme as a source of inspiration was waning, the *Perceval* romances belong to the period of genuine popularity, and, in their varying forms, indicate the process of evolution followed by the tale in its development from the *Gawain* to the *Galahad* form. It may be as well to say, for the benefit of readers unfamiliar with the Arthurian tradition, that Gawain is the very earliest of Arthurian heroes, figuring in the pseudo-historic texts which know neither Perceval, Tristan, nor Lancelot, and that a version of which he is the hero cannot have arisen at a period when his fame had become obscured by the growing popularity of knights later introduced into the cycle.

The differing versions of the story, the elements which may be considered permanent as distinguished from those which are variable, and the light which they may throw on the interpretation of the Quest, are points which will be discussed in the next chapter.

CHAPTER III

THE STORY

THE earliest form, so far as the subject-matter is concerned, is, as we have seen, that embodied by Wauchier de Denain in his continuation of the *Perceval*, where it is found among a number of stories having for hero Gawain, his son, or his brother, and attributed to a certain Bleheris, who, Wauchier says, was '*né et engenuïs*' (born and bred) in Wales.

That Bleheris is identical with the Master Blihis, referred to in the *Elucidation* (a text to which we shall have occasion to return later) as the source of the Grail story, is now generally admitted. It is also highly probable that he is the same as the Bréri to whom Thomas, in his *Tristan*, attributes an unrivalled knowledge of

> *les gestes et les cuntes*
> *de tuz les reis, de tuz les cuntes*
> *qui orent esté en Bretaingne;*

> (all the feats and all the tales
> of all the kings and all the counts
> who e'er had been in Britain;)

and who has, independently, been identified with the Bledhericus, ' *famosus ille fabulator* ' (that famous story-teller), to whom Giraldus Cambrensis refers as having lived not long before his time.

Mr. Edward Owen, of the Cymmrodorion Society, has recently published evidence in favour of the view that this personage may well have been identical with a Welsh prince, Bledri ap Cadivor, living between the years 1070–1150, who, for some unknown reason, threw all his influence on the side of the Norman invaders, and whose name appears in charters in company with Norman knights, in the form of Bledhericus Latinarius, or ' the Interpreter.' According to Mr. Owen, " it is possible that a section of the *Brut y Tywyssogion* (Brut of the Princes), dealing with events in which he took a personal share, may also be from his pen."

This identification, though plausible, is not absolutely proved, but in any case we now know that the earliest extant form of the Grail story came from Wales, and we have reasonable ground for supposing that it was due to a writer who had passed away a quarter of a century before Chrétien de Troyes composed his Grail poem, and who, in his lifetime, enjoyed an unrivalled reputation as a retailer of popular tales and traditions.

The story, which is only a short one, judged by the standard of mediæval tales, relates how Guenevere, and certain of her knights, have gone to a cross-road in a forest, to await the return of the king from a warlike expedition. In the dusk of the evening an armed knight rides past the tents, without drawing rein, or saluting the queen. Guenevere, incensed, sends Kay after him, to demand his return; displaying his usual rough discourtesy, and lack of tact, Kay is unhorsed, and returns to the queen with bitter complaints of the stranger's rudeness. Guenevere now dispatches Gawain on the errand, who, also in keeping with his character, addresses the stranger courteously, and begs his return as a personal favour. The stranger, whose name is never given, demurs, on the ground that he rides on a quest that will not brook delay, and which none but he can achieve; but when Gawain, revealing his identity, pledges his honour that no evil result shall befall him, he consents to return and pay his respects to the queen.

Before, however, they can reach the camp the knight utters a piercing cry, and falls wounded to death by a dart cast by an invisible hand. With his dying breath he bids Gawain don his armour, and ride on the quest, which he, perchance, may achieve. The steed will carry him aright. Burning with shame and indignation at this outrage on his knightly honour (he had promised the knight safe conduct), Gawain sets forth. He rides through a terrible night of storm and tempest, in the course of which he shelters in a mysterious chapel, where a Black Hand, appearing from behind the altar, extinguishes the light, and hideous voices make lamentation.

Gawain's steed, terrified, carries him away, and we are told that but for his valour and worth the knight would have died, but this is

> *du ségré du Graal,*
> *si fet grant pechié et grant mal*
> *cil qui s'entremet de conter*
> *fors si comme il doit aler.*

> (of the secret of the Grail,
> he commits a great sin and a great wrong
> who undertakes to tell the tale
> otherwise than as it should run.)

By the morning Gawain has passed the bounds of Arthur's kingdom; he rides all day through a land waste and desolate, and at nightfall comes to the seashore; he sees a causeway, arched over by trees, leading out into the water, and washed over by the waves; at the end glimmers a light. Gawain would fain draw bridle, and wait for the day, but the steed, taking the bit in its teeth, dashes down the path, and carries the knight to the lighted doorway of a castle.

Here Gawain is received with great rejoicing, the folk assuring him they have long desired his coming; he enters, and is disarmed, when those around know him for a stranger—"this is not he whom we thought" —and they leave him alone.

In the centre of the hall Gawain now sees the body of a gigantic knight on a bier, covered with a crimson silk, a sword on his breast, and lighted candles at head and foot. A procession, headed by a cross of silver, enters, and clergy sing the Vespers of the Dead amid general lamentation. This over, tables are spread for a feast, the king of the castle, entering, greets Gawain kindly, and places him beside him, then follows the mysterious appearance and service of the 'rich' Grail, commented upon above (p. 8). Gawain is filled with awe and astonishment. The feast over, all disappear, and Gawain is again left alone. He now sees a lance, fixed upright in a silver cup, from the point of which flows a continuous stream of blood, which is carried by a spout of emerald into a golden tube, and so without the hall.

While Gawain is looking at this the king enters, leads him to the bier, and, taking up the broken sword, bids him fix the two halves together, which Gawain fails to do. Shaking his head, the king tells him he cannot achieve the quest on which he has come thither. He leads him to another chamber where there are other knights, and tells him he may be able to return at some future time, but none who fail to rejoin the sword can achieve the

purpose of the quest.   Nevertheless, Gawain
has shown such valour in coming thither
that he may ask what he will and he shall be
answered.   He asks concerning the Lance ?
It is the Lance of Longinus, and shall bleed
till the Day of Doom.   Of the Sword ?   It
is the Sword of the Dolorous Stroke, by which
Logres and all the country were destroyed.
The king will tell who smote the blow, and
who was slain by it ; but, as he begins to
speak, weeping the while, Gawain, wearied
out with his journey, falls asleep.   He wakes
the next morning to find himself on the
seashore, his horse tied to a rock beside him,
and no trace of the castle to be seen.   But
now the land is no longer waste, but green
with verdure ; and as he rides on his way, all
the folk bless and curse him ; for by asking
of the Lance he has partially restored the
land (" for so soon as Sir Gawain asked
wherefore it bled thus freshly, the waters
flowed again through their channels, and all
the woods were turned to verdure ") ; had
he asked of the Grail the land would have
been completely restored.

This is a very curious story, complete and
picturesque in its details, and, as we shall see,
capable of an adequate and coherent explanation.   Certain of the *Perceval* MSS.
interpolate, at an earlier point, another visit
by Gawain to the mysterious castle, when
the king is an old man lying on a couch, and

there is a formal Grail procession, consisting of a youth bearing the bleeding Lance, a maiden with a little silver platter (*tailléor*), a maiden, weeping bitterly, who carries the Grail (here not an automatic object) in her raised hands (we are told Gawain does not know what it is she carries), and four serjeants with a bier on which lies a dead body, and a broken sword. The adventure ends, similarly, with Gawain's failure to rejoin the two halves of the weapon, his slumber and awakening in the morning to find himself alone, this time in a morass. This version has evidently been contaminated by the *Perceval* form.

In *Diu Crône*, Gawain, who has ridden long in search of the Grail, comes at last to a goodly land, "like unto a garden, green, and of right sweet odour, it might well be held for an earthly Paradise." He passes a castle of glass, the entrance to which is guarded by a fiery sword, and eventually meets Lancelot and Calogreant ; the three together come to the Grail Castle. In this version the king is old, to all appearance ill, and is found in a goodly hall, all bestrown with roses, for it is summer-time. His vesture is white, cunningly wrought with diaper work of gold, and he is watching two youths playing chess when the knights enter. Gawain is made to sit by the host on a cushion of rose-coloured silk. When the feast is set, Gawain and his

companions are plied with wine, the former
having received a previous warning, refuses
to drink; Lancelot and Calogreant drink
freely, and fall asleep. When the Grail procession enters, Gawain recognizes the Grail-
bearer as the maiden who had previously met
and warned him if he ever saw her again, with
other maidens in her company, not to fail to
ask what they did there. So soon as he puts
the question the king springs up with a cry of
joy; he was dead, but retained a semblance of
life till the Quest was achieved. At daybreak
he and his knights vanish, and only the Grail-
bearer and her attendants remain. They
were the only living beings in this dwelling
of the dead, and this was the cause of their
grief, which has previously been emphasized.

A third version, found in the prose *Lancelot*,
where Gawain fails, and is punished in a
degrading manner for his failure, is noticeable,
first, for its reference to the non-material
character of the Grail, quoted in Chapter I.,
and, secondly, for the fact that during the
night Gawain sees twelve maidens who weep,
and make bitter lamentation before the door
of the chamber from which the Grail issued
forth. Later on the significance of this
incident will become apparent.

To summarize the main features of the
Gawain Quest: it differs from the *Perceval*
in being much more varied in incident and
setting; and in the facts that: (*a*) Gawain

is never related to the lord of the castle ;
(*b*) the Grail is always invested with a peculiar
character of mystery (save in the *Diu Crône*
we do not know what it is, nor of what
material, if any, it is wrought) ; (*c*) the
presence of weeping women, the Grail-bearer,
or others is always insisted upon ; (*d*) there
is always the presence of Death—either there
is a dead body on a bier, or the king himself is dead.

The *Perceval* romances, on the other hand,
though numerous, exhibit far less variety of
detail, so far as the Visit to the Grail Castle
is concerned ; it seems highly probable that for
this incident all derive, in various measure
of directness, from one source. Whether
dwelt upon with elaborate and charming
detail, as in the *Parzival,* or passed over
lightly, as in the prose romances, the initial
setting of the *Perceval* story is the same. It
is the tale of a lad, whose father has died
before, or shortly after, his birth, and who
has been brought up in the woods by his
widowed mother, far from the haunts of
man, and in ignorance, not only of all knightly
accomplishments, but in some instances of
the very existence of human beings other
than his mother and himself. Chance throws
certain knights of Arthur's court across his
path, and, fascinated by their appearance,
he leaves his mother, against her will (thereby
in some versions causing her death), and

presents himself, generally in the roughest garb, and with the most primitive equipment of steed and weapons, before the king, peremptorily demanding knighthood at his hands.

His arrival coincides with an insult inflicted on king and queen by an hereditary foe; the boy follows, slays the insulter, and, donning his armour, rides off on a series of adventures of which the Grail visit forms one. This introductory section affords scope for most poetical treatment, and, in the *Parzival* especially, it is worked out with extreme charm. The lad's love for the singing birds, his mother's jealousy which results in orders to trap them, orders revoked on seeing her boy's grief, the mother's religious teaching—all are admirably told.

> "Then the boy spake: 'Now, sweet my mother, why trouble the birds so sore?
> Forsooth, they can ne'er have harmed thee, ah! leave them in peace once more.'
> And his mother kissed him gently: 'Perchance I have wrought a wrong.
> Of a truth, the dear God Who made them He gave unto them their song,
> And I would not that one of His creatures should sorrow because of me.'
> But the boy looked up in wonder: 'God, mother? Who may God be?'
> 'My son, He is Light beyond all light, brighter than summer's day,
> And He bare a Man's Face that we men should look on His Face alway.

Art thou ever in need of succour?   Call on Him in
  thine hour of ill;
And be sure He will fail thee never, but will hear
  thee and help thee still.
Yet one there is dwelleth in darkness, and I wot men
  may fear him well,
For his home is the house of falsehood and his kingdom the realm of Hell.
Turn thy mind away from him ever, nor waver
  between the twain,
For he who doubteth, his labour shall ever be wrought
  in vain.' "

Compare also the *naïveté* with which the
lad inquires the meaning and use of the
knights' armour :

" Then he handled with curious finger the armour the
  knight did bear,
His coat of mail close woven, as behoveth a knight
  to wear.
And he spake as he looked on the harness: 'My
  mother's maidens string
On their chains, and around their fingers, full many a
  shining ring,
But they cling not so close to each other as these
  rings which here I see.
I cannot force them asunder, what good are they
  then to thee?' "

Of this part of the tale, entirely independent of any Grail interest, we have not
only a version of the *Perceval* story itself, in
the English *Syr Percyvelle of Galles*, where
there is no trace whatever of the Grail adventures, but also versions where the hero
is known under another name, such as the

' Lai ' of *Tyolet*, the early Italian poem of *Carduino*, and the Celtic lay of *The Great Fool*. The introductory section also of the poems which treat of the adventures of Gawain's son, Guinglain, or *Li Beau Desconus*, bear such a resemblance to the *Perceval* '*enfances*' that a common original for the two has been postulated. The story is a charming and popular folk-tale, vivid and picturesque, and nowhere more so than in the form directly connected with Perceval. That hero always preserves throughout his career a certain atmosphere of vigorous and untamed manhood, which is particularly interesting. Perhaps the most individual hero of mediæval romance, Perceval is never as complete and polished a knight as are Gawain, Tristan, or Lancelot ; even in romances entirely apart from the Grail cycle, we find allusions to his curious abruptness and taciturnity. He is a fascinating and picturesque figure, and in his zeal for righteousness he may be ' a true knight of the Holy Ghost,' but from the chivalric point of view one could hardly call him ' a verray parfit gentil knight.'

The setting of the *Perceval* Grail adventure varies, as suggested above, very little. In the poems of Chrétien and Wolfram, the hero, after leaving Arthur's court, finds his way to the castle of an old knight, who receives him kindly, and, shocked at his lack of knightly

breeding and accomplishments, does his best
to impart to him a measure of skill in arms
and courtesy of manner—being far more
successful in the former than in the latter
attempt ! In both poems much is made of
the lad's obedience to certain counsels given
him by his mother, to the strict letter of
which he rigidly adheres, till they are somewhat modified by the old knight's advice,
which, in its turn, is taken for a rule of
conduct.

After leaving the old knight, Gurnemanz,
or Gornemans, he comes to the castle of a
maiden, who proves to be niece to his late
host. She is besieged by an unwelcome
suitor, and almost reduced, through famine,
to the point of submission. In the night she
comes to Perceval's couch, and beseeches
aid ; he consents, overthrows her enemies,
and either betrothes himself to, or weds, the
maiden. After a more or less prolonged stay
at her castle he determines to seek his mother,
and rides forth with that object.

Towards nightfall he comes to a water
where he sees men in a boat fishing ; he asks
shelter for the night, and is directed by the
senior of the men to a castle which he finds
after some considerable difficulty. He is well
received, and conducted to a hall, where he
finds his host, who is identical with the old
man of the boat, lying on a couch ; he is
suffering either from the effects of a wound

(Chrétien and Wolfram) or of extreme old
age (prose *Perceval*). He is made welcome,
and in the poetical versions presented with a
mysterious sword, sent by the niece of the
host ; which sword will break either in a
peril foreseen by him who forged it as one of
three weapons—he never forged more (Chrétien), or if used to deal a second blow
(Wolfram). In both poems this sword is a
perplexing feature ; and the only solution of
the problem seems to be that from the first
there was a sword in the Grail story, the
significance of which, as time went on,
ceased to be understood, and each writer
accounted for the weapon as he thought
best.

Tables are spread for a feast, and a procession enters, preceded by a youth bearing
a Bleeding Lance, the sight of which awakens
a storm of lamentation. In the procession
figure a silver *tailléor*, or two *tailléors*, silver
knives (Wolfram), lighted candles, and the
Grail, which varies between Chrétien's vague
' something ' of gold and precious stones,
Wolfram's Stone, the Lance and Cup together
of the *Perlesvaus*, and the Dish of Borron's
Perceval. There is a mysterious connection
between the Grail and the feast, most clearly
emphasized by Wolfram, who asserts that
the Grail provides the guests with the food
and drink preferred by each ; but in no case
does the Grail possess any such automatic

power as we found in the *Gawain* form. Nor
is there any dead body on the bier; that
feature seems, in the *Perceval* texts, to have
been replaced by the Maimed King, borne on
the litter. There are never any Weeping
Women in the *Perceval* versions, nor, saving
in the incomplete conclusion given by
Wauchier to the story, is the hero asked to
resolder the sword as a test of his fitness to
learn the meaning of the marvels he beholds.
In fact, Perceval never attempts to ask for
an explanation, a failure accounted for by
the instructions he has received from the old
knight, who has warned him against asking
questions. In Gerbert's version, which, as
mentioned above, is inserted between Wauchier and Manessier, he is represented as having,
like Gawain, partially achieved the quest, and
by so doing restored the rivers to their
channels, thereby earning the blessings of the
folk; but in the overwhelming majority of
the texts his failure is absolute and complete, he requires a second visit to achieve
his task.

One important point of divergence from
the *Gawain* form is that Perceval is always
closely related to the Grail King, being either
his grandson, or his nephew. The relationship may be on the mother's side, as in
Chrétien and Wolfram; on the father's, as
in Borron; or on that of both, as in the
Perlesvaus. Gawain, on the contrary, is no

relative.   The significance of this point will
be discussed later.

The fact that Chrétien left his poem unfinished, thus recording the first and abortive
visit only, and that the three writers who have
essayed a conclusion show a bewildering
diversity of tradition, renders the conclusion
of the original *Perceval* Grail poem a highly
problematical question.   The English *Syr
Percyvelle* alluded to above, in which there
is no mention of the Grail, concludes with
Perceval's reunion with his mother, whom he
takes to his wife's castle (here, as in Wolfram,
he marries the besieged lady), and his subsequent journey to the Holy Land, where he
dies.   But how did the first *Perceval* Grail
poem end ?   What was the precise form of
the question he asked ?   Was it, or was it
not, connected with an attempt to mend a
broken sword ?   The king was certainly
cured, but was he restored to youth, as from
Wolfram and Borron there is reason to think ?
And did, or did not, the land share in the
revival of the king ?   It is difficult from
the versions before us to give a decided answer
to these questions.

Thus, to sum up, we have as distinctive
notes of the *Perceval* Grail version : (*a*) the
picturesque *enfances* of the hero, always
present in the story, though not always related
in detail; (*b*) the fact that he always finds the
lord of the Grail Castle engaged in fishing,

which points to a stage when it was thought
necessary to explain, *tant bien que mal*, the
title of the ' Fisher King,' and, we may sur-
mise, to a period when the real meaning of
that title had been largely forgotten ; (*c*)
that the Fisher King is his near relative ;
(*d*) that he suffers under serious physical
disability ; (*e*) the presence of a more or less
stately and elaborate procession of which the
Grail forms a part—we may term it a ' Solemn
Entry of the Grail ' (in Wolfram this procession is of a most gorgeous character) ; and
(*f*) lastly, the absolute failure at his first
visit of the Quester. It will be seen that,
while this is a much more developed form, it
adds nothing of real importance to the story.

In the version of which Galahad is the
hero, the Quest, so far as he himself is concerned, is a quest in name only. His mother
is the daughter of the Grail King, and herself
the Grail-bearer, who, through a ruse practised by her old nurse upon Lancelot, who
believes the lady to be Guenevere, is enabled
to fulfil the prophecy which has marked her
out as the mother of the predestined Grail-
winner. Galahad has grown up, first at the
court of Corbenic, then in a cloister, under the
very shadow of the Grail ; he knows perfectly what it is, and where it may be found.
His first appearance at Arthur's court is
coincident with that of a sword, fixed in a
block of marble, which Galahad alone can

withdraw—an incident borrowed from the *Merlin*, where it forms the test which conclusively proves Arthur's claim to the crown. Here, as remarked above, all the knights take part in the Quest, and when, after a long series of adventures to which a forced symbolical interpretation is given, Galahad returns to Corbenic, he is accompanied by Perceval (who is here no longer a relative of the Grail King, Galahad having supplanted him in this *rôle*) and Lancelot's cousin, Bors. They are joined at the castle by nine other knights, whose names are not given, and who play no further *rôle* in the story. The twelve hold a mystic feast (the Grail King and his son being excluded), at which the Grail, here identified with the Holy Eucharist, yet, as we saw above, still possessing its original automatic, food-providing powers, appears, and by command of Heaven the three Arthurian knights follow it to the land of Sarras. Finally the Grail is received up into Heaven, and never seen again of man.

It is evident that this version can in no way assist us in determining what was the original character and significance of the Quest. It is a definite *terminus ad quem*; and the real problem is to decide how, and by what stages, a story which made its first appearance in the wild and picturesque setting of the Bleheris-*Gawain* form, arrived in the course of development at this highly ecclesiasticized version. The gulf between the two is tremendous, yet both are genuine Grail stories. That the *Galahad* form could possibly represent the original conception and have become transmuted into the *Gawain* is absolutely impossible. There is but one link between the two, the automatic, food-providing powers of the talisman, and that is precisely a feature which strikes us as out of harmony with the general tone and symbolism of the *Galahad* Quest. What, then, is the germ in that wild elusive folk-tale which rendered it of kinship with, and capable of development into, this presentment of Catholic sacramentalism in its most material form ? What is ' the Secret of the Grail ' ?

CHAPTER IV

THE CHRISTIAN THEORY OF ORIGIN

MODERN interest in the legend of the Grail, and the literature in which that legend is enshrined, may be said to have found its starting-point in San Marte's (A. Schulz) modern German edition of the *Parzival* (1836–42), and the accompanying detailed study on the sources of the legend. His work was followed by Simrock's better known translation, with full notes and a discussion of sources. A few years later M. de la Villemarqué published his well-known studies on Breton legend and folk-lore (1846), and from this date onward editions of the texts, and studies on their probable inter-relation and ultimate source, followed on each other with bewildering rapidity.

It would be quite impossible, and indeed out of place, here to attempt a sketch of the development of this critical literature, its inclination first to one solution, then to another, the deflection of interest first into one side channel, then into another, as subsidiary and isolated parallels were seized upon and exaggerated into issues of primary importance.   But it must be borne in mind that, apart from editions and translations of the texts, and *travaux d'ensemble*, there have been published countless brochures dealing with this or that point in the story, some of them, such as those by Dr. Paul Hagen, being works of considerable critical value.   The incomplete character of the MS. evidence, and the fascination of the subject-matter, offer an irresistible attraction to the research student (unfortunately also to the irresponsible and ingenious amateur !), and theory has followed upon theory with the resultant effect of a complex which none but a specialist will care to grapple with.   Could any one find the leisure and the patience necessary to draw up, and tabulate, a complete statement of all the theories on the subject which have seen the light of day, there is no doubt that the result would be a highly entertaining piece of literature.

For those desirous of obtaining a general view of the question, the two most useful works are still Professor Birch-Hirschfeld's *Die Sage vom Gral*, and the late Mr. Alfred Nutt's *Studies in the Legend of the Holy Grail*, both of which contain full abstracts of the texts comprising the cycle, and a discussion of preceding works on the subject. They are specially interesting because the results arrived at differ, and represent the

two main theories of origin—the Christian
and the Folk-lore. The late Professor
Heinzel's study, *Die Alt-Französischen Gral-
Romanen,* is less accessible, and though displaying a far wider range of learning than
either of the other works, suffers under
serious disadvantages of style and method ;
Professor Heinzel had little or no sense of
literary form, and presented the result of his
researches in a series of disconnected notes
rather than as a carefully considered and
organized whole. The work is extremely
difficult to read, and while essential for the
specialist, would drive an amateur to distrac-
tion. A small pamphlet published by Mr.
Nutt (in the little series of ' Popular Studies
on Romance and Folk-lore '), *The Holy Grail,*
gives the results of later investigation, but
does not contain the abstracts included in
the earlier volume.

One point, however, must be borne in view
with regard to these works, *viz.* the fact that
the discovery of Bleheris as an authority for
early Arthurian tradition is of quite recent
date, being the result of an investigation into
the *Perceval* romances undertaken by the
present writer during the years 1902–05, and
made public first in the pages of *Romania*
for 1904, and then in vol. i. of *The Legend of
Sir Perceval* (1906). Previous to that discovery the position of Gawain as Grail hero
had been either altogether ignored, or treated

as of very minor importance ; *e.g.* Mr. Nutt considered him merely as an understudy to the main hero, Perceval.   The fact that, as Dr. Brugger, the leading German critic of Arthurian literature, has frankly admitted, we must henceforth take the Bleheris-*Gawain* form as our starting-point of investigation, must necessarily affect, more or less radically, theroies constructed in ignorance of the importance of this version.

As a brief summary of the controversy, we may say that, till within the last six or seven years, scholars were divided into two sharply opposed camps.   The one held that the Grail story was a purely Christian ecclesiastical legend, the work of monkish compilers, its starting-point being the tradition of Joseph of Arimathea, and his connection with the Vessel of the Last Supper, used later as a ' Saint-Sang ' relic.   From this germ all later developments, however complex, proceeded.

The advocates of the opposing theory maintained that the Grail, far from being a Christian relic, was simply the automatic, food-providing talisman of popular tradition, and as such, of purely Folk-lore, preferably Celtic, origin.   This latter view, in one form or another, is really the older, as both San Marte and Simrock inclined toward it; but the theory of a specifically Christian origin, adopted by Birch-Hirschfeld, has for so long held the field that it may be well to discuss it first.

The latest, and quite a recent, development of this theory is that proposed by Professor Burdach and enthusiastically adopted by Professor Golther, which sees in the Grail procession simply the Eucharistic procession of the Eastern Church; as Golther puts it, "What Perceval sees is the Byzantine Mass." But how the Byzantine Mass came to be celebrated in Northern France (for Professor Golther is one of those whom the mere suggestion that any one but Chrétien de Troyes can be responsible for the Grail story, reduces to incoherent indignation; the question, for him, cannot even be discussed), and in an ordinary castle hall; or in what mysterious manner this Mass differs from that at which Perceval assists in the Hermit's cell, on Easter-Day, these distinguished authorities omit to explain.

But the obviously ' airy ' nature of this last phase of the theory is a fair illustration of its character as a whole. In the opinion of the present writer the theory of the Christian origin of the story, in any form whatever, can only be met by a direct and uncompromising negative. As a simple matter of fact there is no ecclesiastical story which connects Joseph of Arimathea with the Vessel (Dish, or Cup) of the Last Supper; ecclesiastical tradition, as such, knows nothing whatever of the Grail.

Mediæval writers knew this well enough. As early as 1260 the Nederland poet, Jacob van Maerlant, in his *Merlin,* denounced the whole Grail history as mere lies, on the specific ground that the Church knew nothing of the story; and the chronicler Helinandus, speaking of the *Joseph* Grail tradition, remarks naïvely : " *Hanc historiam Latine scriptam invenire non potui* " (I was not able to find this story written in Latin). The story of Joseph's imprisonment by the Jews is indeed recorded in the pseudo-*Gospel of Nicodemus,* or *Acta Pilati,* but there is no mention of the Grail in that text. Any reader familiar with the Art Galleries of Europe will recognize that while Joseph of Arimathea and Nicodemus are constantly to be found in representations of the Deposition from the Cross, or Burial of our Lord, nowhere, not even in an anecdotal *predella,* is there a record of Joseph and the Grail. The story is the creation of romance, not a legend of the Church.

Nor, leaving the incidents of the story aside, can the Grail in any way be claimed as a genuine relic. As Dr. Brugger has very acutely remarked, such relics are ' *besucht, nicht gesucht,*' their whereabouts is well known and widely advertised ; they are objects of pilgrimage and profit to the church or city fortunate enough to possess them. If there ever had been a genuine Grail Saint-

Sang relic, that relic would have been as well located, its fame as widely spread, as the kindred relics of Bruges and Fescamp, or the *Volto Santo* of Lucca.   There is more than a possibility, indeed, that it was precisely the great reputation of the Fescamp relic which provided the initial suggestion and inspiration for the formation of a kindred tradition at Glastonbury.

As those conversant with the literature are now well aware, the Fescamp ' Saint-Sang ' relic, like the *Volto Santo* of Lucca, is connected with Nicodemus ; he it was who collected the Sacred Blood, he who carved the wondrous Crucifix, both were miraculously transported by water to their present shrine.

The fact that the canonical Gospels record the interview of Nicodemus with our Lord would probably account for his being, in early Christian tradition, a more important figure than Joseph, concerning whom we have no such evidence ; even the text upon which the whole fabric of the *Joseph* Grail story is based is the Gospel, not of Joseph, but of Nicodemus.   The Wauchier continuation, speaking of a certain adventure of Perceval, refers as authority to a text to be found at Fescamp :

> *si com le conte nus affiche*
> *qui a Fescans est toz escris—*
>
> (as the tale assures us
> which at Fescans is fully written—)

a passage which seems to point to a possible
Perceval Grail story, connected with that
Abbey. The fact that Fescamp possessed a
guild of minstrels attached to its foundation,
would render possible the construction of such
a story, based on a combination of the popular Folk-tale of Perceval, and the Grail theme ;
a combination which, given the antecedent
identification of the Grail with a Saint-Sang
Vessel, would fall quite within the limits of
reasonable hypothesis. Such a compilation
might well ante-date any of our existing texts.

The presence of the ' Saint-Sang ' relic at
Fescamp is affirmed in a treatise on the
subject dedicated to the third Abbot, who
died in 1107 ; thus it was certainly there by
the end of the preceding century. All the
legends connected with the building point to
the Abbey as having been founded to contain
the relic ; there is no tradition of the relic
having been brought to an already existing
Abbey.

The Minstrel Confraternity, according to
its charter which is still in existence, was
founded by the first Abbot, who died in
1031 ; and it may be assumed, from parallel
instances, that such a Confraternity, even
as the similar body connected with Saint
Guillaume du Desert, was organized with the
initial aim of spreading the reputation of the
Abbey, and its relic. Thus inferential evidence would point to the early years of the

eleventh, or even to the closing years of the
tenth century, as the starting-point for tales
dealing with the Fescamp relic.

On the other hand, the connection of
Joseph of Arimathea with Glastonbury was
a tradition of late and slow growth. There is
no doubt that, from an early period, Glastonbury was associated by tradition with the
Celtic Avalon. A curious story was told of a
certain Glast, or Glasteing, who, having lost
his (here, eight-footed !) swine, found them
on this spot under an apple tree. The old
British name for apple being *avalla*, he named
the place *Insula Avalloniæ*, the marshes which
surrounded Glastonbury rendering possible
the description of the spot as an island.
According to William of Malmesbury it was
also known as *Ynis-gwitrin*, the *Isle of Glass*
(also a name for the Other-world), and the
name Avallon, the chronicler remarks, may
have been derived from that of the earliest
inhabitant, Avalloc.

It is perfectly clear that early writers, while
identifying Glastonbury with the old Celtic
Paradise of Avalon, or the Isle of Glass, had
no real knowledge of the origin of the name;
but the place must, already, in pre-Christian
times, have enjoyed a local reputation for
sanctity; it was most probably the site of
an early Celtic temple, or a burying-place.
The Glast story is of Irish origin, and, in the
opinion of M. Ferd. Lot (' Glastonbury and

Avalon,' *Romania*, vol. xxvii.), was attached
to the place by Irish monks ; but one thing is
quite certain, no early writer bases the fame
of Glastonbury upon the ground of its association with the earliest foundation of Christianity, through the person of a contemporary
of the Redeemer.

The first mention of Joseph of Arimathea,
in this connection, is based upon an interpolation in a passage drawn from the Chronicle of Freculf, who states that S. Philip and
S. James sent forth twelve of their disciples
to convert the island of Britain ; the chronicler quotes Josephus as his authority.   In
some twelfth-century MSS. Joseph appears
as leader of the band ; a change which may
be due either to the misunderstanding of a
copyist, or the desire to have a well-known
name for the leader.   The interesting fact
that the apocryphal *Gospel of Nicodemus*,
which, as stated above, gives an account of
the imprisonment of Joseph by the Jews, was
well known in Britain in the eighth century,
whereas it was not generally current on the
continent till some four hundred years later,
would explain the popularity of Joseph in
these islands, and the reason why, when a
special Conversion legend was demanded, he
should be selected as hero.

At first the Christian Abbey of Glastonbury was content to base its claims to honour
on its being the burial-place of certain Irish

and Celtic saints. By the end of the eleventh century it had fallen on evil days, and lost much of its renown. To recover its prestige, and in order to provide a bulwark against the growing power and authority of Canterbury, the monks set to work to fabricate a series of diplomas and charters, purporting to be the grants of early British and Saxon kings. In the twelfth century Glastonbury became a veritable bureau for the fabrication of fictitious deeds of this character. Finally the monks set the seal to their audacity by claiming to be the earliest Church founded in Britain.

Now when we take into consideration the fact that the two Abbeys of Fescamp and Glastonbury belonged to the same Order; that the first was under the special protection of the Norman kings, by whose ancestors it was founded; that there was constant communication between Fescamp and England (under the first Abbot a member of the royal —Saxon—family of England was a member of the Order; the second Abbot visited the court of Edward the Confessor, and received donations from that monarch, afterwards confirmed by his successor; the fifth Abbot, Henry de Sully, was nephew to King Stephen), —when we have thus, on the one side of the water Fescamp, with Nicodemus, the Saint-Sang, and Holy Fig-tree, it seems to me that the genesis of the corresponding sequence on

the other side of the channel, Glastonbury,
Joseph, the Grail, and the Holy Thorn, is not
far to seek !

No direct evidence of this dependence
exists, but the texts of the *Perlesvaus*, as we
now possess it, show distinct signs of a
mingling of the traditions. The conclusion
of the story states that the original Latin
source was found " in the Isle of Avalon, in
a holy house of religion that is placed at the
head of the adventurous marshes, there,
where lie King Arthur and Queen Guenevere "
—a description which points unmistakably
to Glastonbury, but can hardly antedate the
official ' discovery ' of the tombs of Arthur
and his queen, towards the end of the reign
of Henry II., *i.e.* within the last twenty years
of the twelfth century.

At the same time this very romance, and
this romance alone, traces the hero's genealogy to Nicodemus, as well as to Joseph; he
descends on the father's side from the former,
on the mother's from the latter. We noted
in the previous chapter that the *Perlesvaus*
occupies a peculiar position in the literature
of the cycle, showing traces of early origin
combined with very late features ; it has
certainly undergone more than one redaction,
and the theory that we have here an early
Perceval Grail romance, originally constructed
at Fescamp, and later worked over in the
interests of the fellow-foundation at Glaston-

bury is not one that should be lightly dismissed.

Is it not clear that, had Glastonbury really possessed a treasure of the twofold sanctity to which the Grail, as alike Vessel of the Last Supper and Saint-Sang relic, could rightfully lay claim, the monks who, as history proves, were not slow to make capital of all that might bring fame to their Abbey, would certainly have exploited that treasure for all that it was worth ? But when we consider the fact that, on the contrary, Glastonbury never asserted its possession of a relic that entitled it to rank, as a goal of pilgrimage, with the shrines of Fescamp and Lucca (I instance this latter as the Grail texts themselves refer to it), it seems to me that the whole weight of evidence is in favour of the *Joseph* Grail story being a mere literary invention of the latter part of the twelfth century, inspired by the famous tradition of Fescamp, and based upon a romance originally constructed by the minstrels attached to that foundation.

Another point which should not be ignored is that the Grail is a Saint-Sang relic in appearance, rather than in fact. Contrary to what might, and ought, to be expected, the interest of the story is centred on the Vessel, the container, not on its content. The Legend, the Romances, are the *Grail* legend and romances. Now Grail, to the

minds of twelfth-century writers, most undoubtedly meant a Dish; the very MS.
which gives us the best version of the *Gawain*
Grail story, in a section by the same hand,
relates how Gawain arrives at a certain
castle during the temporary absence of its
lord, and finds a meal prepared awaiting his
return. Among the viands are ' boars'
heads on grails of silver.' Helinandus, in
his chronicle referred to above, describes the
Grail as a Dish, ' wide and somewhat deep.'
Evidently, then, in the Grail legend, we
are dealing with a tradition which centres
round a Vessel, independent of what that
Vessel may contain. Even when the *contenu*
is the most sacred thing on earth, the Blood
of the Redeemer, the importance of the vessel
is such that it still dominates the situation ;
it is the Grail story after, as before.

It is obvious that later writers felt this
difficulty ; the talisman first took the prefix
of ' Saint,' the ' Saint-Graal,' which was later
written as one word, the ' Sangraal.' Finally,
the ingenious etymology, Sang Réal, the
Royal Blood, was adopted as explanatory of
the title. All eminently satisfactory, so long
as the original texts were unknown or ignored.
But they, unfortunately, lend no support to
this ingenious theory ; rather do they
contradict it, for they invariably give the
word without a qualifying adjective, without
even always the definite article. Chrétien

speaks of ' *uns Gréaus*,' a Grail, and Wolfram
von Eschenbach knew it as a 'Stone.' We
have no genuine Holy Blood relic here.

Further, the Grail possesses attributes not
to be harmonized with the hypothesis of a
genuine Christian origin. No recorded Saint-
Sang relic, most certainly no Eucharistic
chalice, comes and goes in automatic fashion,
leaving rich food and drink in its train. Yet
even in the Galahad *Queste*, where the Grail
is surrounded by a halo of Christian sanctity,
its appearance at Arthur's court· means that
" every knight had such meats and drinks as
he best loved in this world." (It would be
interesting to know if Professor Golther
holds this for a feature of the Byzantine
Liturgy ?)

And no hypothesis of a Christian origin
can explain the *mise en scène* of the story :
the lonely castle by the seashore (be it noted,
it is always a castle, never a temple ; only
in the very latest forms of the story is the
Grail kept in a chamber which might not
unfitly be described as a chapel); the Waste
Land, only to be restored with the restoration
of the King ; the Dead Knight ; the Wailing
Women ; the outburst of grief which ac-
companies the appearance of the Lance.
No, however attractive the theory of a
Christian origin for the Grail story may appear
at first sight, it breaks down at every point
when critically investigated. This special

solution of the problem must be dismissed, not merely as ' not proven,' but as thoroughly and completely discredited. Whatever the Grail may be it is not a Christian relic ; whatever the source of the story, it is not an ecclesiastical legend.

CHAPTER V

If, then, the advocates of the Christian Grail theory have thus signally failed to make good their contention, how does the matter stand with regard to their opponents, the advocates of a Folk-lore origin ?

We may at once admit that they can put forward a much stronger, and better reasoned, case. If their attempt to solve the problem cannot be held to have fully succeeded, it is rather because the solution proposed is inadequate to meet all the conditions, than that, like the Christian, it is radically unsound.

Thus, the advocates of the Folk-lore Talisman, those who hold the Grail to be *ab origine* what the German scholars term a *Wunsch-Gefäss*, can point to countless folk-tale records of similar food-supplying vessels, some, too, of a mythic rather than of a popular origin. Such was the cauldron of the Dagda, from which none ever went away unsatisfied, connected with the Tuatha de Danann, the mythical, semi-divine ancestors of the Irish race. Such, again, was the cauldron of Bras, in the *Mabinogi of Branwen the Daughter of Llyr*, which possessed the power of restoring the dead to life.

Or there is the mysterious and venomous Spear, the *Luin* of Celtchar, which emitted streams of fire, and required to be constantly plunged in a cauldron of blood, to quell its venomous attributes.

The Four Treasures of these mysterious Tuatha de Danann were the Stone of Destiny, which proclaimed the future king; the Sword; the Spear; and the Cauldron, above referred to—talismans corresponding with singular accuracy to those of the Grail Castle.

Again, advocates of this theory have no difficulty in proving the folk-lore and traditional character of a tale such as the *Perceval enfances*, a tale which, as the late Mr. Alfred Nutt, following in the steps of J. G. von Hahn, has shown, finds its parallels amid all the Aryan peoples. It is, indeed, easy to go further, and demonstrate the general use of popular folk-tale themes in the evolution of that body of romantic literature to which the Grail texts belong. Thus, *The Three Days' Tournament*, a story in which the hero appears three consecutive days in different armour, a theme found all over the world, is used over and over again in Arthurian romance, and there is strong reason to believe that it was this story, in one of its

most popular forms, which gave the initial
suggestion for the immortal loves of Lancelot
and Guenevere. The *Lanval* story, of the
love of a knight for a fairy mistress, of which
we have many variants, the story of *Carados
and the Serpent*, the story of *Merlin*—all
these are notable instances. Small wonder,
then, that the theory of a folk-lore, and of a
specifically Celtic folk-lore, origin for the
Grail legend, has won widespread acceptance.

And yet this theory cannot be said to
satisfy, fully and completely, the conditions
of the problem. The weak points, and unfortunately they are points of supreme
importance, may be stated as follows :

If we cannot accept the theory that a
definitely religious and Christian object
could be credited with the attributes and
methods of procedure of a mere food-
providing talisman, it is equally difficult to
accept the converse—that a purely Folk-lore,
food-providing vessel should be identified
with the most sacred objects of the Christian
Faith, the Blood of the Redeemer, the Chalice
of the Eucharist; and that, not in stories
which might be the result of popular growth
and ignorant misapprehension (there are no
Christian Grail folk-tales), but in lengthy and
detailed romances, obviously the work of
knowledge and intelligence. This is a point
which, as a rule, the advocates of this particular theory prefer not to face. They postu-

late the non-Christian, preferably Celtic,
origin of the tale and suggest certain varied
theories of that origin ; they admit the
definitely Christian character of the later
forms of the romance, but the gulf between is,
as a rule, left unbridged.

Professor Wechssler did, indeed, some years
ago, attempt to fulfil the required conditions
by postulating a version of the *Joseph of
Arimathea* story, in which that hero was
miraculously sustained during his forty years'
captivity by an automatic, food-providing
talisman, which, for some unexplained
reason, received the name of Grail; but he
omitted to explain why, if this were the
case, all mention of the talisman should have
been omitted from the texts recording this
captivity. This idea he then combined with
a reconstructed version of the story, in which
the hero's name was Galahad, but the incidents were those of the *Perceval* form. Here
again we were left in ignorance of the process
by which the name of the later hero became,
permanently and indissolubly, attached to
the primitive incidents, while the genuine
hero was provided with an entirely new story,
not one incident of the original tale remaining
to his credit ! The whole was complacently
offered as a *via media*, which should solve all
the contradictions and difficulties, of the
cycle. The result was generally held to do
more credit to Professor Wechssler's ingenuity

than to his critical faculty, but the attempt is in itself a proof of the extreme complexity and difficulty of the problem.

Thus, while admitting the full force of the folk-lore parallels and the validity of the argument as regards many features of the story, we are compelled to ask, what, granting the initial postulate, there could have been about this special food-providing talisman that differentiated it from the great family of similar talismans ? Why should this, more than any other of its countless fellows, have been so speedily, so radically, Christianized, and surrounded with such an atmosphere of mystic secrecy ? This is a point which cannot possibly be evaded ; it is a point which has never been fairly met.

The second main objection is that here, even as in the Christian theory, the *mise en scène* is not satisfactorily explained. No one has as yet brought forward a folk-tale corresponding in incident and setting to the Grail story. Explanations are indeed suggested for isolated features. Thus, the Dead Knight on the bier has been paralleled with Arthur in Avalon ; the Maimed King (with reference to Wolfram's explanation of the character of the injury) to Kronos, in his Western Isle ; the Waste Land, to an incident in the *Mabinogi of Manawyddan, the son of Llyr*. But these are all independent the one of the other ; a story that corresponds

in any detailed manner with either the
Bleheris-*Gawain* story, or the Grail section
of the *Perceval*, is so far unknown. This is
the more suggestive in that, as Dr. Griffith
has recently shown, there exists a well-
marked group of folk-tales curiously parallel
in incident and intention with the opening
phases of this latter form—the forest educa-
tion of the hero, his dramatic appearance at
court, the slaying of the Red Knight, etc. The
hero follows a well-marked traditional path
for the first part of his adventures; but that
path never leads, as were the theory sound
it surely should lead, to the Grail Castle.

It is, of course, possible that certain of my
readers may here ask, But what of the evidence of the *Perronik* ? Have we not here
a genuine folk-tale, parallel to the *Perceval*-
Grail story ? Have we not here the Dümm-
ling hero, the Lance, and the Basin, or Cup ?
M. De la Villemarqué thought he had found
the source here, and his view has recently
been revived and warmly championed by
Professor von Schroeder.

Now there is no doubt that in the *Perronik*
we have a popular tale belonging to the
'Great Fool' group; *i.e.* the hero is certainly a near relation of Perceval. Also, the
talismans he wins are strongly reminiscent of
Lance and Grail. But in my view 'reminiscent' is precisely the right word to use;
they were suggested by these objects, they

are not the objects themselves, far less are they their source. There are two unmistakable notes of a late origin which have escaped the notice of those enamoured of the tale. The manner in which alone the giant can meet his death brings the tale into the well-known group of the ' Hidden Soul,' of which it is clearly a late variant. The fact that the giant is slain through the agency of the embodied Plague, the ' Yellow Death,' and also the references to the bells ringing for the Feast of Corpus Christi, are proofs that this particular version of the tale is later than the introduction of these two features into Europe. Neither were known before the thirteenth century.

The weak point, and it is a fatally weak point, of the method employed by the defenders of both Christian and Folk-lore theory, is that both alike content themselves with a discussion of the nature and origin of the Grail, and its attendant talisman, the Lance, each, as it were, *per se*, and independent of the other, and disregard, more or less, the setting in which they are placed. Yet surely no theory of the origin of the story can be considered really and permanently satisfactory, unless it can offer an explanation of the story as a whole ; of the relations between the two chief talismans, and of the varying forms assumed by the Grail : why it should be at one time a Food-providing object of unexplained form, at another a Dish; at one moment the receptacle of streams of Blood from a Lance, at another, the Cup of the Last Supper; here 'Something' wrought of no material substance, there, a Stone; and yet everywhere and always possess the same essential significance; in each and every form be rightly described as *The Grail*?

As a rule, this, the real essence of the problem, has been evaded. Criticism has been content to find independent and unrelated solutions for this or that aspect of the Talisman; yet it is always and everywhere the Grail, and between its varying manifestations some definite principle of relation should surely subsist.

The late Mr. Alfred Nutt endeavoured to find a solution of the main difficulty in a combination of two distinct *Quest* stories, termed by him the *Feud* and the *Unspelling* quests. The first would give us the Dead Knight, the Sword, and the introductory section of Manessier's conclusion of the *Perceval*, where the hero must avenge the death of the Fisher King's brother on his slayer, before that personage can be healed. The second would account for the question which, rightly asked, brought about the restoration alike of King and Land. This latter feature Mr. Nutt connected with the Irish *geasa*, or taboo, restrictions laid upon a hero to do, or refrain from doing, certain things.

But it is surely unnecessary to postulate a combination of themes, unless we are absolutely certain that no single hypothesis can adequately meet the case.

The task, then, which modern scholarship must deliberately face is that of co-ordinating the varying versions of the legend, and evolving a theory which shall explain, not merely one form of the Grail, but all the varying forms, while at the same time it provides an adequate explanation for the story-setting. In the opinion of the present writer there is one theory, and one alone, which will, naturally, and without undue forcing of the facts, explain the apparent enigma of the Vessel and its surroundings, and do justice to what is really sound and enduring in the earlier and opposing theories of origin; for in the Folk-lore theory, at least, there is much that is sound. This, which we may perhaps designate the *Ritual* theory, we will now proceed to examine.

CHAPTER VI

THE RITUAL THEORY

THE theory to which we are now about to devote our attention was first suggested by the present writer, in vol. i. of *The Legend of Sir Perceval* (' Grimm Library,' vol. xvii.), and subsequently developed in a paper (' The Grail and the Rites of Adonis ') read before the Folk-lore Society, and published in vol. xviii. of *Folk-lore*. It was still more fully treated in vol. ii. of *The Legend of Sir Perceval*. The suggestions made in these works have, on the whole, been very favourably received, and while there has been a hesitation to accept, in its entirety, the suggested process of development, the initial principle, has, in many quarters, been accepted as a sound basis of criticism.

As we have noted above, the weakest point in both Christian and Folk-lore theories is that both alike fail to explain the combination of elements in the problem to be solved. On either hypothesis the presence of features permitting, nay, inviting, the formulation of the opposing theory is a very grave objection. Thus, if the Grail were a purely Christian Vessel, it ought not to behave like a mere food-providing talisman; if it were a mere food-providing talisman, it ought not to be surrounded with the atmosphere of mysterious sanctity befitting the holiest of relics. The very existence of such contradictory elements in a form that can neither be ignored nor considered unjustified by the texts, demands the formulation of a theory that shall, by harmonizing the apparent contradictions, at once explain, and justify, their existence. The only view that will meet the case is to regard the Grail as something which, while pre-Christian in origin, was an object of reverence and awe, something which *ab initio* was found in such surroundings, was put to such a use, that its Christianization, and subsequent identification with the holiest symbols of our Faith, could be brought about by a natural development from within, rather than by a forcible imposition from without.

Modern investigation, and the growing recognition of the importance of the comparative study of religion, have in recent years familiarized us with forms of faith and practice the knowledge of which was earlier confined to specialists, and, further, have connected such forms of faith with modern survivals of popular custom and superstition in a manner hitherto little suspected.

In the light of modern research, we now know that the most widespread method of symbolizing the annual natural processes of growth and decay was that which regarded the animating Spirit of Nature under an anthropomorphic form. The name of the god varied in different lands; the earliest form of the cult which has left distinct traces is the Babylonian, which knew the deity as Tammuz; but the best known form, and that which has, in fact, persisted to our day, is that which, taking its rise in Phœnicia, spread through the Greek Islands on to the mainland, and gained so strong a hold on the Greek peoples that it was carried afield by them, and became especially popular in their Egyptian colonies.

Here the god was known as Adonis (from the Syriac, *adon*, ' lord,' thus not really a proper name, but an appellative), and was figured as a fair youth, the beloved of the goddess Aphrodite. Dying a violent death, as the result of the chase of a wild boar, he descended to the Nether-world, where he became the lover of the queen of Hades, Persephone. Aphrodite, by her passionate entreaties, prevailed upon Zeus to restore her lover to life; and henceforward Adonis shares his existence between the Upper and the Lower world, as the consort now of Aphrodite, now of Persephone.

Thus, while in the spring the return of

Adonis to life, and his union with the goddess, was welcomed with every sign of popular rejoicing, his annual departure to the Shades was the signal for widespread mourning, of a character and intensity that has left a peculiar and enduring mark upon popular tradition.

The relation of the two component parts of the celebration varied.

Sometimes the return of Adonis was celebrated first ; this was the case at Alexandria, where the nuptials of Adonis and Aphrodite were celebrated with the greatest pomp and display. After two days an image, representing the god (sometimes merely a head, made of papyrus), was committed to the waves, and a period of mourning, varying from three to seven days, followed.

In other places the death of the god took precedence, and was followed by feasts celebrating his restoration to life. This latter seems to have been the more widely spread form of the cult, and that corresponding the more closely to the survivals in modern folk-custom.

It is not essential for the purposes of this study to cite numerous examples of such survival. Those desirous of a fuller acquaintance with the subject have only to turn to the pages of Mannhardt's *Baum- und Feld-Kultus* or Frazer's *The Golden Bough*, to find more than sufficient proof of the enduring character of these rites, but the following examples will illustrate my meaning.

Thus in Lausitz, on Lætare Sunday, women, veiled as mourners, carry a figure of straw, dressed in a man's shirt, on a bier to the bounds of the next village. There they tear the figure to pieces, and hang the shirt on a young and flourishing tree, which they cut down and carry home with rejoicing. In the Lechrain a man is dressed in women's clothes, laid on a bier, borne by four men, and bewailed by men dressed as professional women mourners, ' *Klageweiber.*' In this guise he is carried to the village dung-heap, where he is thrown down, drenched with water, and buried in straw. More striking still is the Russian custom. Here the Vegetation Spirit is named Jarilo, and represented by a doll, with phallic attributes. The figure is placed in a coffin, and carried through the streets at sunset, by men, while drunken women surround the procession, making lamentation in the following remarkable terms : " Of what was he guilty ? He was so good. He will rise no more. Oh ! How can we part from thee ? What is life to us when thou art no more ? Arise ! If but for a moment. But he arises not, he arises not ! " Finally Jarilo is laid in the grave. These examples, selected from among innumerable parallels given by Mannhardt, are sufficient to show the persistent character of these ceremonies, and the attendant features.

But what is of especial importance for the purposes of this investigation, is the fact that it is precisely this form of nature-ritual which in its earlier, and more ceremonial, shape, provides us with a series of incidents closely corresponding to the *mise en scène* of the Grail story. Thus the dead body on the bier, the Maimed King on the litter, correspond with the god, dead, or wounded in such a manner that he is deprived of his reproductive powers. This is an analogy which has hitherto been too much ignored, though certain scholars have evidently been aware of its existence. Vellay and other writers point out that the term ' thigh,' used in connection with the wounding of Adonis, is merely a well-recognized euphemism, of which they give numerous instances; and, while the majority of the Grail texts employ this term for the wound of the Fisher King (*parmi les cuisses*), Wolfram von Eschenbach uses words which leave us in no doubt that here, as elsewhere, the term is to be understood in an euphemistic sense.

Thus we can now understand how the wasting of the land can be connected with, and directly caused by, the death, or infirmity, of the King, and how the achievement of the Quest, by restoring to health (and some of the Grail romances specifically state, to youth) the personage upon whose vitality the vitality of the land depends, can restore these wastes to verdure. Some of the texts, *e.g.* the Bleheris-*Gawain* form, and the Gerbert continuation, say quite clearly that the achieving of the Quest has restored the rivers to their channels, and caused the dried-up waters to flow. This is precisely the feat which our earliest Aryan forefathers ascribed to their divine hero, Indra ; the ' Freeing of the Waters ' is the greatest boon that can be bestowed upon man.

Now, too, we understand the insistence upon the mourning in general, and specifically, the importance assigned to the *rôle* of the Weeping Women. The position assigned to them in these celebrations was one of such prominence that an Arabic writer of the tenth century gave to these rites the name of *El-Bugât* or ' The Festival of the Weeping Women.' The terms in which Vellay, in his work on Adonis, describes their demeanour, " *elles sanglotent éperdûment pendant les nuits,*" parallel closely the experience of Gawain as recorded in the prose *Lancelot*, where, in the middle of the night, " Sir Gawain hearkened, and heard the sound of bitter weeping and lamentations, he deemed well 'twas the voice of women," and beholds twelve maidens, " who made the greatest lamentation in the world," kneeling before the door of the chamber wherein the Grail has entered, they " made prayers and orisons, and withal wept bitterly."

The interest of this passage lies in the fact that there is absolutely no reason for mourning of any kind here ; the Fisher King is in full possession of his powers, the Grail is the Grail of the Galahad *Queste*, and the dwellers at Corbenic have everything that heart can desire. This trait can only be explained as a survival from an earlier form the real significance of which has been forgotten. In a lengthy passage interpolated in the *Perceval* MS. of the Heralds' College, we are told that as one result of the successful achievement of the Quest, the hero shall learn " why the maiden who carries the Grail weeps ceaselessly." But in the poem to which this is an addition (Chrétien's), the Grail-bearer does not weep ! No unprejudiced critic of the Grail literature can avoid the conclusion that in the Weeping Women of the texts we have a feature the true meaning of which is no longer understood by those who record it.

Again, the fact that, alike in classical times and in modern survivals, the figure representing the Spirit of Vegetation is thrown into the water (into the sea, at Alexandria), will enable us to understand why the Grail Castle is invariably described as situated on the sea-coast, or the banks of a great river.

It is not too much to claim that, alike in incident and intention, the ritual of the Adonis

cult provides us with the only real parallel
to the *mise en scène* of the Grail story we have
so far discovered.

But what of the Grail itself ? If we take,
as its primary form, that which it bears in the
Bleheris-*Gawain* story, that which, as we have
noted, recurs over and over again in persistent
and perplexing fashion, even in the latest
and most highly Christianized forms, that of
a food-providing Vessel, a *rich* rather than
a *holy* Grail, it may well have been, in the
first instance, the Vessel of the general ritual
meal, which formed a part of these celebrations. This would account at once for
the fact that it supplies food, and food of a
specially rich and varied character. Why,
however, it should be regarded as automatic,
is a question less easy to answer.

We do not know precisely, in fact we
know very slightly, what really took place at
these feasts ; but we do know that priests
of these early faiths were often credited with
magical, or miraculous, powers, which the
science of later days has explained by their
possible skill in mesmeric, or hypnotic, arts.
It is thus quite within the bounds of possibility that the service of these ritual feasts
may have been marked by what, to the
simple-minded participant, bore the character of the marvellous ; and within the bounds
of possibility, too, that a Vessel bearing such
a character should gather to itself as accre-

tions, traits characteristic of the many food-providing talismans of folk and fairy tale. But while these nature-cults, in their simple and popular form, may very well explain the origin of this 'feeding' Grail, it must be admitted that they do not, in that popular form, provide an explanation for its puzzling mutations. For an explanation of these we must examine the material from another side.

In this branch of our investigation we are treading on less well-assured ground. The existence of these cults, their wide-spread character, their persistent survival, even to the present day, the close parallel between their ritual and the incidents of the Grail story—all this, the initial basis of the Ritual theory of origin, is now very generally accepted by scholars, in fact it would be difficult of denial. But the further steps, the road followed by the tradition in its development into a Christian mystical romance, are so far a matter of hypothesis, and can be presented only as such. Yet, to readers of this Series, the hypothesis, in view of the character of the facts and ideas with which it deals, may be expected to commend itself as essentially probable and satisfactory.

A point which cannot be overlooked in connection with these nature-cults in general, and with the Adonis ritual in particular, is the marked prevalence during these cele-

brations of practices which, to our modern
views, are alike repellent and reprehensible.
But to our forefathers the bond uniting men
with Nature was far closer than it is with us.
The vital force which animated both was one
and the same, actions which issued in the
reproduction of human life might reasonably
be looked upon as calculated to stimulate a
vigorous growth in Nature.

That this idea survives to the present day is
amply demonstrated by the curious, and to
our minds unedifying, practices which constantly accompany these ceremonies, and of
which abundant evidence can be found in the
books referred to.   To sum up the position in
a few words, ' sympathetic magic ' is an element the presence of which in all these cults
must be held as fully proven.

Thus the Adonis and kindred cults were
essentially ' life ' cults, their aim being to
preserve the life of the land, and of the folk
dependent upon its fruits.   But it is quite
obvious that while the general public might
rest content with the outward expression—
the public mourning and rejoicing, the ritual
feast—and regard the whole celebration
simply as a means of securing fruitfulness—
even as the Italian peasant of to-day looks
upon the successful performance of the ceremony of the *Scoppio del Carro* (an undoubted
nature-ritual survival) as a means of ensuring
an abundant harvest—and be content with

that, the priests assigned a different, and
higher, significance to these ceremonies.
Vellay does not hesitate to assert that these
rites had an inner, an esoteric, meaning. He
says :

"*Les fêtes publiques n'en sont qu'une
parade extérieure, et comme artificielle*" (of
which the public did not understand, were
not meant to understand, the inner significance), "*mais au delà, le sens esotérique,
l'essence mythique, pour ainsi dire, s'y cris-
tallise dans la tradition rituelle des prêtres.*"

He goes on to remark that, at the moment
this double current becomes historically
noticeable (the popular side as shown in the
feasts, the esoteric in the teaching of the
priests), the rise of the Orphic doctrine had
given to the earlier traditions a new life and
a deeper meaning. At the same time, the
Greek philosophy, carried to Alexandria, had
there come into contact with Egyptian legend
and religion, and under this influence has
assumed a character at once more subtle and
more profound. To put it concisely, Vellay
is clearly of opinion that, at a certain stage of
development, the Adonis ritual assumed the
character of a mystery.

In the first of a series of most interesting
articles, contributed to *The Quest*, and dealing
with ceremonial game-playing in church, a
practice which survived into late mediæval
times, Mr. G. R. S. Mead remarks that

" the ancient higher mystery-institutions had two main grades ; in the lower were shown the mysteries of generation, or physical birth and death ; in the higher, the mystery of regeneration, or of spiritual birth and life " (vol iv. p. 109).

If we apply this principle to the cult under discussion, and postulate that the Adonis rites, elevated to the rank of a mystery, conformed to this model, the presentation of the Grail in a three-fold form becomes easily explicable. The basis of instruction was of course the outward ritual, in which all the worshippers unite, the central feature of which is the sacramental meal of which all alike partake. This gives us the Grail in its primary form as Dish, the Grail as described by Helinandus.

In his Chronicle, speaking of the revelation of the Grail made to a certain hermit in Britain, Helinandus explains the term as follows : " *Gradalis autem, vel Gradale, Gallice dicitur scutella lata, et aliquantulum profunda, in* ˚*qua preciosæ dapes divitibus solent apponi gradatim, unus morsellus post alium in diversis ordinibus.*"

Does not this description in all its details fit admirably into the conception of the central dish of a ritual feast, food of a rich and special quality, arranged on the dish in regular order, being offered to the worshippers, one morsel apportioned to each ?

I have already pointed out that, to the French writers of the twelfth century, *Grail* did, most undoubtedly, connote *Dish.* Here, then, we have the Grail as Feeding Vessel, the ' rich ' Grail of the Bleheris-*Gawain* form ; it is the dish in which food of a rich and varied character is offered to the worshippers.

But to those elect who desired to penetrate beneath the outer symbolism of the ritual to its inner and hidden meaning, the Grail, the Source and Food of Life, assumed a different form.   Passing in natural sequence from the lower to the higher, the aspirant would first be initiated into the mystery of the origin of physical life ;   and at this stage he must certainly have undergone a test corresponding in character with the instruction for which it was a preparation.   In the Bleheris-*Gawain* form we learn that the hero, on his road to the castle, finds, and enters, a mysterious chapel, where a Hand, black and marvellous, extinguishes the Altar light, and hideous voices make lamentation ; we are told that the hero was in danger of death, but of these marvels no one dare speak, for they appertain to ' the secret of the Grail.'

Now it is a point which has not yet been sufficiently studied, that a visit to a Perilous Chapel, or Cemetery, is found in many of the Grail romances ; the details differ, but the adventure is always described as perilous in the extreme.   In the *Perlesvaus* this *motif* is

developed in a most curious and significant
form.   Arthur, intending to ride forth with
early morning, has bidden his squire prepare
horse and armour over-night and be ready to
ride with him at dawn.   The squire does this,
and lies down to sleep in the hall.   In his
dream he imagines that he has overslept himself, and that the king has ridden forth
without him.   He rises, and follows in haste,
coming, as he thinks, to a Chapel in a
Cemetery wherein are many coffins.   In the
Chapel lies a Dead Knight, on a bier, with
tapers in golden candlesticks burning at
head and foot.   The squire takes one of the
golden candlesticks, and rides on after the
king.   In the forest he meets a black man,
armed with a knife, who, on his refusal to
give up the candlestick, smites him in the
left side.   The unfortunate youth awakes, to
find himself lying in the hall at Cardoil,
wounded to death, with the golden candlestick beside him !

Now 'initiations' can, and do, take place
while the aspirant is physically in a trance
condition ;   and it seems to me by no means
impossible that this curious story may be
the survival of a genuine Grail tradition.
When Perceval faces the adventure of the
Chapel, as he does in Manessier, the Dead
Knight lies on the Altar, and he has to sustain
the onslaught of a demon, black and hideous
in the extreme.

I think we shall not go far astray if we conclude that the test preceding, and qualifying for, initiation into the secrets of physical life, consisted in being brought into contact with the horrors of physical death, and that the test was one which might well end disastrously for the aspirant.

Gawain had passed this test satisfactorily before his arrival at the Grail Castle, and is congratulated by the King on the valour which has enabled him to reach that goal.   After he, with other inhabitants of the castle, has partaken of the common feast, and been served by the ' rich ' Grail, he is left alone in the hall, and then, and not before, he sees the Vessel in its lower aspect, as a Cup, or Vase, receiving the blood which flows from an upright Lance. Vase and Lance, in this conjunction, are well-known phallic symbols, the Vase, or Cup, representing the female, the Lance, or Spear, the male element, while the blood is the Life.

This, the lower aspect of the esoteric teaching, then, supplies us with a second form of the talisman, the Cup, explains its association with the Lance, and, by the introduction of the blood flowing from the latter, prepares the way for the ' Saint-Sang ' developments.

The final stage is the initiation into the higher Secret of the Mysteries, that of regeneration and spiritual life.   It is quite

obvious that here the experience must, of
necessity, pass on a higher, a non-material
plane, and the source of spiritual life must be
other than a material, food-supplying Vessel.
And so we have the ' Holy ' Grail, which,
we are told, was " not of wood, nor of any
manner of metal, nor was it in any wise of
stone, nor of horn, nor of bone, and therefore
was he (Sir Gawain) sore abashed." The
Grail, at this stage, is wrought of no material
substance. The test here demanded of the
Quester is that he shall ask concerning the
nature and use of this mysterious Vessel ;
but, as we have seen, he does not ask, often he
falls asleep, and though instruction may be
given, his ears are closed. Frequently, as in
the Bleheris-*Gawain* form, he is required to
re-weld a broken sword ; his failure to do this
debars him from achievement.

Is it a far-fetched hypothesis to assume
that here the Sword represents the will-
power, which, welded to its hilt, the ' pentangle,' the mystic symbol which is supposed to
give power over the Other-world, will enable
the initiand to undergo the final test, that of
retaining his consciousness during the Vision
of the ' Holy ' Grail, so that, the Vision passed,
he can, in full and clear remembrance of what
he has seen, demand without fear of denial
what this mysterious Vessel is, and whom, or
what purpose, it serves ? As students are
well aware, the Sword of the Grail romances is

a very elusive and perplexing feature. It takes upon itself various forms ; it may be a broken sword, the re-welding of which is an essential condition of achieving the quest ; it may be a ' presentation ' sword, given to the hero on his arrival at the Grail Castle, but a gift of dubious value, as it will break, either after the first blow, or in an unspecified peril, foreseen, however, by its original maker. Or it may be the sword with which John the Baptist was beheaded ; or the sword of Judas Maccabæus, gifted with self-acting powers ; or a mysterious sword *as estranges ranges*, which may be identified with the preceding weapon. In this later form we find that the scabbard may bear the mysterious inscription, ' *memoire de sens* ' (the sense memory), and one of the finest of our Gawain romances, *Sir Gawain and the Green Knight*, assigns to that hero, as his distinguishing badge, the ' pentangle.' Thus it seems to me that the interpretation suggested above, though verging on the ' occult,' yet lies well within the acknowledged facts of the story.

This, then, in its main outlines, is the Ritual theory. And I think any fair-minded critic will admit that it fulfils the conditions of the problem in a manner which the older theories failed to do ; for it explains, quite naturally, the incidents, and *mise en scène* of the tale, and accounts for the divergent, and at first sight, contradictory, forms assumed by the talisman. This last is a point to which sufficient importance has hardly been attached. Scholars have been too apt to exercise a capricious selection between the different forms of the Grail, and to decide in favour of the originality of that which best conforms to the conditions imposed by their particular theory ; but all and each is *The Grail*, and any sound theory of origins must recognize and admit them as such.

Other considerations lend further weight to the proposed interpretation. It is a curious, and on other grounds inexplicable, fact that there is a persistent tradition of three Grail Kings. The *Perlesvaus* designates the three as the *Roi Pescheur*, the *Roi de Basse Gent*, whose name was Pelles (probably a later addition), and the *Roi del Chastel Mortel*, in whom there was as much of evil as in the others of good. Chrétien and Wolfram know two kings : the lord of the Grail Castle in their versions uniting the characters of Fisher, and Maimed, King, while his old father, preserved alive in extreme old age by the sight of the Grail, or by a ' host ' contained in it, duplicates this latter *rôle*. In a unique MS. of the Arthurian cycle, an extended *Merlin*, preserved in the Bibliothèque Nationale (Fonds Français, 337), the three kings are Alain, Pellinor, and Pelles, all of whom are ' Maimed.' In the prose versions we find generally the king Pelles, his

old father, and his son Eliezer, who, however,
never succeeds as King and Guardian of the
Grail.

The tradition has become hopelessly confused and intricate, but it appears to point
to an earlier stage at which each manifestation of the Grail was under the charge of
an appropriate Guardian. In the esoteric
interpretation this Guardian would represent
the Life-Principle, and whereas the Maimed
King would correspond closely with the Dead,
or Wounded, God, and in this character be
present at the general ritual feast, the Fisher
King, representing that personage in his full
activity, would have charge of the spiritual
Vessel, the ' Holy ' Grail. The King of the
Chastel Mortel, which term can hardly connote other than the Body, the Flesh, would be
Keeper of the Grail in its lowest form ; and
that this was indeed his *rôle* is indicated by
the fact that, in the one text in which this
character has been preserved, the *Perlesvaus,*
he is making war upon the Fisher King for
possession of the Lance and the Grail—his
own symbols which have here become Christianized and removed from his keeping.

The title of ' Fisher ' King, as applied to
the Guardian of the Grail, is a somewhat
perplexing element in the tradition. The
symbolism is beyond any doubt a ' life '
symbolism. The Fish is a well-known emblem
of life, and is found alike in pre-Christian,

and Christian, iconography, while the title of
' Fisher ' has been bestowed upon more than
one early divinity.   Thus Adapa the Wise,
the son of Ea, of Babylonian myth, is the
' Wise Fisher ' ; Buddha, is ' The Fisher ' ;
it may be also Orpheus.   The connection of
this special symbolism with the form of
nature-worship under discussion is not very
clear.   The popular survivals of the Adonis
cult have preserved no trace of this nomen-
clature, and it may be that the title belongs
exclusively to the esoteric ' mystery ' development which has given us the Grail
tradition.   But two points are assured : (a)
the ' fish ' symbolism is a ' life ' symbolism ;
(b) a personage bearing the title of ' Fisher ' is
never a mere man, it is a divine title, and
the person bearing it is either a divinity, or
the representative of a divinity.   Regarded,
then, from the ritual point of view, it seems
clear that the Grail Quest should be viewed
primarily as an initiation story, as a search
into the secret and mystery of life ; it is the
record of an initiation *manqué*.   The Quest,
properly speaking, begins only when the
hero, having failed at his first unpremeditated
visit to the Castle to fulfil the tests to which
he has been subjected, sets out with the
deliberate intention of finding the vanished
Temple of the Grail, and fulfilling the conditions which shall qualify him to obtain a
full knowledge of the marvels he has beheld.

This aspect of the problem had already presented itself to the acute intelligence of the late Professor Heinzel. Although he had not detected the close parallel existing between the Grail incidents and the details of popular nature-ritual, and was further hampered by his prepossession in favour of a Christian origin, yet he saw quite clearly that the peculiarities of the story, the nature of the test employed, the mysterious question, all partook of the character of an initiation, and he expressed his opinion that the story contained certainly as one of its elements the record of a failure to pass an initiatory test.

It is not also without interest, or significance, that readers of romances, unacquainted with the Grail literature in general but familiar with ' occult ' tradition and practice, should invariably detect this element in the story. More than once I have lent a translation of the *Gawain* Grail adventures to friends whom I had reason to believe were familiar with such subjects ; invariably the result has been the same—the book has been returned with the remark : " This is the story of an initiation, told from the outside."

If we accept this solution of the problem, it will lead us to the conclusion that the Grail literature is not to be considered as a cycle dependent upon mere literary invention, the elaboration of a theme due, originally, to the genius of this, or that, poet.

Literary invention has doubtless played a part in the development of the cycle; *e.g.* such a poem as the *Parzival* of von Eschenbach, with its elaborate ' Oriental ' introduction, the charming account of the life led by mother and son in the wood, the amplification of the details of the Grail procession into a gorgeous 'Pageant of Fair Women,' the knightly wanderings of Trevrezent—all this is imaginative literature, and imaginative literature of a high order. But the groundwork of the story, the ' kernel ' of the cycle, is not invention, but tradition ; it is the legendary record of something that really happened, of an experience at once terrifying and exalting, which left an indelible impression upon the mind of him who underwent it. Where that experience was undergone, how and by what steps the record assumed its final and distinctively Christian form, are questions we will discuss in another chapter.

CHAPTER VII

THE TESTING OF THE THEORY AND CONCLUSION

WE see, then, that the Ritual theory of Grail origins, by which we mean the view that sees in the Grail tradition as preserved to us the confused and fragmentary record of a special form of nature-worship, which, having been elevated to the dignity of a 'mystery,' survived in the form of a tradition, offers the most complete solution of the problem hitherto proposed. For, while the sequence of incident in the Grail story corresponds with curious fidelity to well-authenticated forms of ritual procedure, and the result to be obtained is in both cases the same, the 'mystery' development explains, as no other theory has even attempted to explain, the divergent forms assumed alike by the Grail and its Guardian.

It may even be said that the evidence operates in two directions; for if the theory of 'mystery' development accounts for the triple character of the Grail, that triple character, and the persistent tradition of

three Grail Kings, in their turn prove that
the particular form of nature-worship of
which these romances preserve the tradition
must have been something more than the
simple popular celebration, whether mournful
or joyous, with which works on comparative
religion have made us so familiar.

But if we accept this basic hypothesis we
find ourselves confronted with a series of
questions the answer to which is of primary
importance. What, we must ask, was the
path followed by this special tradition in its
evolution from a non-Christian to a Christian
form ?   Where did it originate ?   What were
the influences which converted this, hypo-
thetically, religious, into a romantic theme ?
Who were the personages responsible for the
evolution ?

These questions involve a problem, or
series of problems, of extreme complexity,
and in the absence of direct MS. evidence a
complete and final answer is scarcely possible ;
the line of research is new, and it involves the
consideration of questions the connection of
which with the Grail literature has so far
been but imperfectly apprehended. The
present writer is firmly convinced of the
essential soundness of the views here set
forth, but at the same time holds that, at
the present moment, they can only be put
forward as theories, and that their definite
establishment and acceptance as facts call

for the co-operation of workers whose interests, and sphere of labour, lie as a rule outside the enchanted fields of mediæval romance.

We have of recent years learnt to recognize the fact that the beliefs and practices of our remote ancestors enshrined a spirit of extraordinary persistence and vitality; that popular custom and practice to-day reflect with startling and curious fidelity the popular custom and practice of the past; we know, too, that such continuity of custom and practice is not purely secular, surviving merely in popular celebrations, but may be found enshrined in the rites and ceremonies of the Church. Where this is not actually the case, the fact that the special folk-practices which are now recognized as nature-cult survivals, coincide frequently, if not invariably, with the ecclesiastical feasts, prove that the Church, where she did not accept and adopt, extended not merely tolerance but patronage.

Thus the *Scoppio del Carro* at Florence, alluded to above, takes place on Easter Eve. At the singing of the *Gloria* at High Mass, a dove enveloped in fireworks flies down a wire reaching from the high altar to a car, stationed outside the great west door, and decorated with fireworks, while it is drawn by white oxen with gilded horns and wreaths of flowers. If the dove flies straight, and

arrives without mischance at the car, igniting
the fireworks upon it, the ensuing harvest
will be good. Should it fail to reach the car,
a bad season may be expected. In many
parts of Germany on Palm Sunday, after the
customary procession, a priest is beaten by
another with rods, branches of willow, etc.
The blow from the 'wand of life' is, as Mannhardt points out, a means of quickening life,
animal and vegetable, and as such is a widespread Spring ceremony. The numerous survivals of the 'Adonis' rites, the carrying
forth, and burial, by mourning women, of
the dead Spirit of Vegetation, and the tri-
umphant bringing in of the young Spirit of
Spring, very generally fall on a Sunday, or
other Church festival such as Whitsuntide.
Such ceremonies are at the root of the surviving Ascension and Rogation-tide pro-
cessions, and readers of *The Quest* will not
need to be reminded of the adoption of pre-
Christian ritual ceremonies, within the very
precincts of the Church, to which Mr. Mead
has drawn attention in his most interesting
articles on 'Ceremonial Game-playing in
Mediæval Churches.' The latter section of
the first of these studies, that dealing with
'The Burial of Alleluia,' is of especial interest
to us, as supplying a most curious and
suggestive ritual parallel to the secular
practices referred to above.

Those familiar with the services of the

Catholic Church, Roman or Anglican, are of course well aware that the festal response ' Alleluia ' is disused from Septuagesima to the Thursday in Holy Week ; but previous to the publication of Mr. Mead's article they were doubtless unaware of the fact that in mediæval times, in French churches, and no doubt elsewhere, *Alleluia* was treated as a feminine personification, and as such solemnly interred and bewailed. I quote an extract from the statutes of the Cathedral Church of Toul, in Lorraine, given by Mr. Mead in the article referred to :

" On the Saturday of Septuagesima Sunday, at Nones, the choir boys are to assemble in the great vestry, in festal attire, and there arrange the burial of Alleluia. And after the last *Benedicamus*, they are to go in procession with crosses, torches, holy water, and incense, and carrying a clod of earth as at a funeral, and are to proceed across the choir, and go to the cloister, wailing, to the place where she (Alleluia) is buried. And after one of them has sprinkled the water, and a second censed the grave, they return by the same way."

Mr. Mead further publishes the singularly beautiful office for Saturday in Septuagesima, wherein Alleluia is invoked in terms which would befit a divine, or royal, personage: " Alleluia, while she is present they entertain her, and they greatly long for her while she

withdraws herself. And for evermore with
head encrowned she triumphs it before the
Lord, Alleluia!" The Abbé Lebeuf, from
whose letters to the *Mercure de France* our
information is derived, recognized that this
solemn burial of Alleluia should be paralleled
by a solemn and joyous ceremony of resur-
rection ; but he states that neither in this
case, nor in that of a similar ceremony where
a top with ' Alleluia' painted round it was
whipped out of the church by a choir boy,
could he find a record of a corresponding
ceremony of reintroduction.

Now who, and what, is this mysterious
' Alleluia,' the time and circumstances of
whose burial coincide so strangely with
the time and ceremonies accompanying
the death and burial of the Vegetation
Deity ?

The history of the liturgical use of Alleluia
by the Christian Church is a subject that
would well repay further study. In a passage
from a treatise of Cardinal Joannes Bona,
cited in the article under discussion, the
phrase, 'the mystery of Alleluia' is employed,
and the modulation of the vowels referred to
as possessing a symbolic value and importance. Such vowel-modulation appears from
the text of a curious, so-called, Mithraic
initiation ritual which has been preserved to
us, to have been a matter upon which much
stress was laid in early mystery-ceremonies,

as being of effectual value in invoking the presence of deity. Mr. Mead connects the sex and personification of Alleluia with the Gnostic personification Sophia, and thus the ' Alleluia' office of the Mediæval Church with the remains of early Gnostic mystery-ritual.

On the other hand, a very curious fact is that the Abbé Lebeuf refers to a specially beautiful MS. of an Alleluia office, as contained in a diptych, inlaid with panels of ivory, yellow with age, on which were to be seen the figures of " Bacchanals, of the goddess Ceres in her car, of Cybele the mother of gods," etc. (it is to be regretted that the good Abbé did not specify further !), thus associating the ceremony with the very group of Vegetation practices we have been examining.

It looks very much as if we had here evidence of a nature-cult, developed upon mystery-lines, and Christianized through the medium of Gnostic ideas. The relation existing between what we may term the higher Paganism and the early Christian Church is a subject to which, so far, in- sufficient attention has been devoted. We are too apt to reflect back our own view, based on the records of mediæval intolerance and modern missionary literature, of the position of those outside the Christian Creed, to the early period of the foundation of our faith, and fail to realize that in those early days Christianity was less the representative of intellect and civilization than of a special ethic and method of relating the present to the future dispensation. The early Fathers of the Church saw no such gulf between Christian and pre-Christian teaching as we now postulate, and in especial they were at pains to show that their own creed was in no way to be contemned on the ground that it made appeal to the uninstructed only. Rather they claim that they are in no way inferior to the older faiths, for if these had 'mysteries' so had Christianity. Saint Clement of Alexandria, in his *Stromata*, uses a form of speech and argument widely opposed to the view of the modern orthodox Churchman. Thus he does not hesitate to assert categorically that our Lord did not "disclose to the many what did not belong to the many, but to the few to whom He knew that they belonged," and that "secret things are entrusted to speech, and not to writing, as is the case with God"; and reiterates more than once the principle that "the Mysteries of the Faith are not to be revealed to all." What form precisely the parallel to the 'higher mysteries' of pre-Christian faiths assumed in the primitive Church is now difficult to ascertain; but there is no doubt that what we now know as Gnosticism enshrines in its few and fragmentary remains the tradition of a great

system of early Christian esoteric teaching
and practice.

There were early Christian mysteries ;
what relation they bore to the higher pagan
teaching we cannot now decide. But, in
face of the fact that Christianity undoubtedly adopted, with little or no change,
customs and practices, some of them of a
very primitive and unedifying character, it is
most improbable that she ignored, or re-
jected, the higher spiritual ' mystery ' form.

Nor does it seem improbable that, given
the adoption of such esoteric beliefs and
practices, the remembrance of them might
be preserved in an incomplete and distorted
form in romantic as in popular tradition.
Such, for example, may possibly be the origin
of the famous tradition of *Saint Patrick's
Purgatory*, a story exceedingly popular in
the Middle Ages and surviving in more than
one mediæval English poem.

This story relates the adventure of a knight
of King Stephen's court, who, after leading a
reckless and dissipated life, made atonement
for his sins by braving the dangers of a
descent into Purgatory, the opening to which
had been revealed in a vision to Saint
Patrick. Owain, the knight in question,
after fasting strictly for fifteen days, was
led by the abbot and monks of the
church wherein the entrance to Purgatory
was found, to the cave, and entering, dis-

appeared from their ken for three days. During this time he traversed the different regions of punishment, and, though in grave danger from the fiends who ruled in this nether world, passed in safety to the Terrestrial Paradise, where he was granted a foretaste of the joys of the Blessed. After the expiration of the three days, he came forth from the cave, attended by a glory of celestial light, a transformed and regenerated character.

Now in the non-Christian, possibly also in Christian, mysteries the culminating point of initiation was reached in a trance, during which the candidate was supposed to pass through the dangers of the lower world and receive definite instruction and enlightenment; the soul, at the expiration of the trance, which sometimes lasted three days, returning, purified and regenerated, to reanimate the body.

The parallel is singularly close; and it is certainly a tempting theory to assume that this popular mediæval story enshrines a reminiscence of an actual experience, possible in early Christian times.

Now is it possible that our Grail tradition also belongs to a similar category, and bears witness to a similar origin?

From the evidence at our disposal, it seems certain that the earliest version of the story came from Wales, and was related by the

Welsh story-teller Bleheris to his French friends and allies. In the case of another *Gawain* adventure belonging to the same group, we learn that Bleheris told it to the Count of Poitiers, with whom that particular tale was a special favourite. Of the early Welsh religion we do not, as yet, know much. We know, however, the Druids to have been nature-worshippers, and that liberality towards them would be rewarded by plentiful harvests; we also know that they taught reincarnation and the immortality of the soul; in fact, there was a tradition to the effect that Pythagoras had been their pupil. There exist collections of early Welsh poetry, the translation and publication of which may possibly throw more light on the precise character of Druidic life-teaching.

But the Welsh were closely akin to the Irish, and the gods of the Celtic pantheon are common to both peoples. Of these early Irish deities, the Tuatha de Danann, we know definitely that they were at the same time Gods of Vegetation and Increase, and Lords and Masters of Life. According to the Irish Annals, they came to Ireland from Greece, and in the wars with the Syrians had aided the Athenians by restoring their slain to life. The late Mr. Alfred Nutt, in his study on *The Voyage of Bran*, terms them 'Masters over the essence and manifestation of Life.'

And the treasures of these mysterious Beings are the treasures of our Grail Castle : Cup, Lance, Sword, and Stone !

Some modern Grail critics have been so much impressed by these facts that they have sought in the Irish tradition the direct source and origin of our Grail stories ; but the parallels are isolated, and nowhere do they present us with a sequence of incident that can be accepted as the basis of our stóry. There is most certainly a common tradition at the root of both ; but direct interdependence has not, so far, been proved.

If we consider that we have a tradition that the deities worshipped alike by Irish and Welsh were of Greek origin; that popular belief in both lands connected a system of agricultural nature-worship with belief in the immortality of the soul and a form of reincarnation or rebirth; that survivals of the particular form of nature-worship most popular in Greece are found in these islands—it does not seem too far-fetched an hypothesis to suggest that this latter cult may have been known also in its 'mystery' form, and, surviving the introduction of Christianity, have been secretly practised in lonely and inaccessible districts in Wales ; the mountain glens and fastnesses of that country offering a shelter to the worshippers of a dying faith.

The Grail texts lend support to this theory.

Certain MSS. contain a very curious and fragmentary text, to which allusion has been made above, bearing the hitherto very perplexing title of *Elucidation*. It is now found prefixed to the *Perceval* of Chrétien de Troyes, and has been treated by scholars as an introduction to that poem, presumably by a later hand. This text professes to have for authority a certain 'Master Blihis,' a personage of whom for many years critics knew nothing, but who in the light of recent discoveries can hardly be other than Bleheris. It purports to give the origin of the Grail tradition, and, from the close parallels between its version of the incidents and the Wauchier section ascribed to Bleheris, it seems probable that, in its original form, it was composed as a formal introduction to the group of *Gawain* adventures related by that story-teller.

Regarded from the point of view of a Christian origin of the Grail, this text is utterly unintelligible; from a Folk-lore point of view it is interesting, but hardly illuminating; from the Ritual point, however, it possesses features of peculiar interest and significance.

It starts with laying special stress upon the mysterious and dangerous character of the subject with which it deals:

> *C'est del Graal dont nus ne doit*
> *Le secret dire ne conter*

Car tel chose poroit monter
Li contes ains qu'il fust tos dis
Que teus hom en seroit maris
Qui ne l'aroit mie fourfait.

.   .   .   .   .

Car, se Maistre Blihis ne ment,
Nus ne doit dire le secré.

(It is of the Grail of which none should
Tell, or recount the secret;
For such a thing might arise
Ere that the tale was all told
[Or: For the tale, ere it was fully told,
Might stir up that by which]
That men might be grieved thereby
Who yet had not transgressed.

.   .   .   .   .   .

For, if Master Blihis lie not,
None should tell the secret.)

The story would tell how the land of
Logres was destroyed.   Aforetime there were
dwelling in the mountains maidens who
brought forth to the passing traveller food,
pasties, bread, and wine, until King Amangons
did wrong to one among them, took away her
golden cup, and deprived her of her virginity,
an evil example which his knights were not
slow to follow.

Des puceles une esforcha
Et la coupe d'or li toli.

.   .   .   .

Li autre vassal de l'honor
Quant ço virent de lor signor
Qu'il enforçoit les damoiseles
La ou il les trovoit plus beles,

Tout autresi les esforçoient
Et les coupes d'or emportoient.

(He outraged one of the maidens
And took from her the cup of gold.

. . . . . .

The other vassals of his court
When they saw their lord
How he outraged the maidens
There, where he found them the fairest,
They also outraged them
And carried off the cups of gold.)

As a result of this conduct the springs dried up, the grass withered, the land became waste, and the court of the Rich Fisher, which had filled the land with plenty, might no longer be found. The land lies waste for a thousand years and more, till, in King Arthur's days his knights find maidens wandering in the woods, each with her attendant knight. They joust; and one, Blihos-Bliheris (Bleheris?), vanquished by Gawain, comes to court, and tells them that these maidens are the descendants of those ravished by King Amangons and his men, and how, could the court of the Rich Fisher who guards the Grail once more be found, prosperity would return to the land. We may here note that we are told that this Blihos-Bliheris was so good a story-teller that none in Arthur's court were weary of listening to his tales:

Si tres bons contes savoit
Que nus ne se pëust lasser
De ses paroles escouter.

(So very good were the tales he knew
That none could become weary
Of hearkening to his words.)

This recalls the reputation of Bledhericus,
as '*famosus ille fabulator*,' and the fact that
Bréri knew

> *Les gestes et les cuntes*
> *De tuz les reis, de tuz les cuntes*
> *Ki orent esté en Bretaingne.*

(The feats and the tales
Of all the kings, of all the counts
Who e'er had been in Britain.)

As the result of his stories Arthur's knights
set forth on the quest for the vanished court,
and we are told :

> *Mesire Gauvains le trova*
> *En icel tans q'Artus regna*
> *Et fu a la cort par vrété,*
> *Ça avant vos ert bien conté*
> *La joie qu'il i gaegna*
> *Dont tous li regnes amenda.*

(Mesire Gawain found it
In that same time that Arthur reigned.
Further on ye shall be told
Of the joy that he won there
Of which all the kingdom was the better.)

But, we are told, Perceval had found it
first—a manifest addition, introduced in
order to bring the text into some sort of
correspondence with the poem to which it is
the ostensible preface.   An account of the

Grail visit follows, told in close agreement
with the Bleheris-*Gawain* form, the details of
which agree with no *Perceval* visit.   The text
goes on to say that the court of the Rich
Fisher was found seven times, and the
streams ran again, and the land was re-
peopled.   A brief summary of these ' findings '
is given ; each, it is said, has its own tale,
and these tales, it is worth noting, agree in
more than one case with tales included in
the Wauchier continuation.

Now the fact that this text is entitled
Élucidation shows, I think, that to the mind
of the writer it did afford an explanation of
the Grail problem ; but so far that explanation has baffled the acumen of scholars.
It is obvious that from the point of view of
the Christian origin of the story, that which
connects the Grail with Joseph of Arimathea,
there is nothing to be made of it.   From the
point of view of a Folk-lore origin, it is a
fantastic and picturesque story, but one that
cannot be classed as a member of any known
family or group of folk or fairy tale.   From
the Ritual point of view it seems to be capable
of reasonable explanation.

Is it a far-fetched hypothesis to assume
that we have here, couched in figurative
romance form, an account of the disappearance of a once-popular form of faith
and worship ?   That at one time the nature-
ritual, upon the due performance of which the

fertility of the land was held to depend, was celebrated publicly and generally ; but in consequence of the insults offered by a (probably local) chieftain and his men to the priestesses of that cult, or may be to the temple maidens, the open celebration ceased. The tradition of these rites, their significance, and their continued life in some secret stronghold, was, however, preserved in the families of those who had been, perhaps still were, officials of the cult. That Bleheris was a member of such a family, and, therefore, in possession of the Grail tradition which, in the form of a romantic Arthurian tale, he told to his French friends. The tale would thus be, as I have already on other grounds assumed, the traditional record of a genuine experience.

This view seems to me to meet all the conditions essential for the starting-point of our story. In the present state of our knowledge of the Druidic religion we cannot affirm that nature-worship, in a ' mystery ' form, was practised by them ; but neither can we deny it. We do know that they held views on the origin and transmission of life of a profound and complicated character. Also, besides the Greek origin claimed for the Irish gods and the ascertained double character ascribed to them (at once deities of increase and fertility, and lords of life), we have the fact of the Phœnician settlements on

British coasts, which would render possible
the introduction of the Adonis cult by the
original founders.   The postulates on which
our hypothesis rests are, I submit, well
within the bounds of historic possibility.

How, then, is the process of evolution into
a Christian mystical romance to be traced ?
First, I think it is obvious that we have here
the result of two distinct and separate currents of influence.   The material has been
remodelled from the outside by men who had
no knowledge of what the story really meant ;
it has been developed from the inside by
those who possessed that knowledge.

To the first group, the Talisman, in its
lower form, the Cup, accompanied by the
Bleeding Lance, irresistibly recalled the instruments of the Passion.   Be it remembered
that this was the period of the Crusades,
when the whole attention of Christendom
was concentrated on the effort to wrest the
Holy Places, the scene of the Life and Death
of our Lord, from the hands of the Infidel.
Every prince or noble returning from the
Holy Land would bring with him a relic of
more or less pronounced sanctity.   None of
these relics were of more importance than the
Holy Blood, which lent distinction to the
shrines of Bruges and Westminster, and helped
to exalt the reputation of the previously
existing Saint-Sang of Fescamp.   The discovery of the Holy Lance at Antioch, towards

the end of the twelfth century, had given an
impetus to the formation of legends dealing
with its reputed owner, whether centurion
or soldier ; there can be little doubt that
hagiographical details connected with the
Lance of Longinus ultimately affected the
descriptions of the Grail Lance.

The process of Christianization, then,
started at the lowest and most obvious point
of contact, and there seems reason to believe
that at its outset it aimed at, and effected, no
more than the identification of one special
symbol with a Christian relic ; the Bleheris-
Gawain form, in the best version extant,
remaining unaffected save in the identification of the Lance with the weapon of the
Passion ; the Grail itself, and all the details
of the story retaining their original ' popular '
character.   From the interpolations in certain MSS., it seems probable that the next
step was the connection of the Grail, as
feeding - vessel, with Christian tradition,
through the personality of Joseph of Arimathea.   There can, I think, be little doubt
that the model for the Joseph story was
found in the Fescamp legend ; and, as we
have seen above, there is ground for sus-
pecting that the first definitely Christian
Grail romance may have been due to the in-
ventive talent of the Minstrel Guild attached
to that foundation.   It was probably a version of this romance, worked over, and

modified in the interests of the kindred foundation of Glastonbury, which definitely associated the Grail with Joseph, as Apostle of Britain.

We no longer have the *Perlesvaus* in its original form ; and it is not easy to say whether the original author did, or did not, understand his material. The presence of the Three Kings, of the Perilous Chapel, and other minor incidents would seem to indicate that he did; but in its present form the Christian exoteric tradition is dominant. We may note also that the prominent position assigned to Gawain, and the courteous and chivalrous character he bears in the romance, are certain indications of a comparatively early date, even for our redaction ; Lancelot has not yet ousted him from his position as first knight of the court.

At the same time his primacy as Grail hero has already been assailed, and he has been forced to yield in pride of place to Perceval. Whether there ever was a definite Christian form of the *Gawain* Grail Quest is a difficult question to decide. The character of this hero belongs to the very earliest stratum of Arthurian tradition, and is associated with certain mythic conceptions closely akin to those which find expression in nature-ritual, but somewhat difficult to reconcile with Christian teaching and ethic. Gawain is beyond all doubt the original protagonist of the Quest, in its primitive, pre-Christian form ; and it seems most probable that, as such, an attempt was made to retain him in that original position by introducing modifications and interpolations into an already existing story, such as we see introduced into the Bleheris form. But the whole process of Arthurian romantic evolution was in the contrary direction ; Gawain not only could not be retained as Grail hero, but was forced gradually to yield his position as Chivalric hero to other knights. So far as the evidence of the texts preserved to us is concerned, the process of evolution of the Christian Grail Quest is associated with Perceval. Perceval, like Gawain, is originally a Folk-lore hero; unlike Gawain, he never seems to have been connected with the Grail in its pre-Christian form.

I have elsewhere (*Legend of Sir Perceval,* vol. ii.) discussed the question of the reasons determining the choice of Perceval as Gawain's successor ; they are not easy to determine. I am inclined to hold that the determining factor was the recognition of the Grail Quest as an Initiation story, assisted by the fact that Perceval is always known as ' the son of the Widow ' (*le fils de la veve dame*), a well-known title for the initiate. This would, of course, indicate that the author of the original *Perceval* Grail Quest understood the true character of the story; and if that original *Perceval* Quest were, as seems probable, the first form of the *Perlesvaus*, we have on other grounds reason to come to the same conclusion.

On the other hand, there is no evidence that Chrétien de Troyes, to whom one school of critics would fain ascribe the conception and construction of the first Grail romance, had any idea whatever of the real character of the story. There is no trace of any 'occult' significance in his presentation; the fact that while departing from the general tradition in making Perceval's father survive the birth of his son for some years (in the original tale he dies before, or immediately after, his birth), he ascribes to him the wound peculiar to the Fisher King, shows that he was handling his material without accurate knowledge of its character. The more primitive features of the story, the Dead Knight upon the bier, the Weeping Women, are absent from Chrétien's version; and it is to my mind impossible to resist the conclusion that to the French poet the story of the Grail Quest appealed as a romance of chivalric adventure, and as nothing more.

With Robert de Borron the case is different. This writer is certainly later than Chrétien, but as certainly he possessed knowledge which he could not have derived from Chrétien's poem. He knew, and that from the inside, the material with which he was

dealing. To Borron this is no mere nature-
ritual, on the performance of which the
fertility of the land depends. He has retained the threefold symbolism, the three
successive Tables, the three Grail-Keepers,
but he lifts the interpretation on to a higher
plane. For him the Grail is equated with
the Christian Eucharist. There can, I think,
be little doubt that he designed his version
from the point of view of one familiar with
Christian esoteric teaching, one to whom
the threefold aspect of the Grail naturally
translated itself into the threefold significance of the Eucharist, as the Feast of
Communion, the actual Body and Blood of
the Lord, and the source of Spiritual Life.
It is more than possible that Borron was one
of those who would have joined with full
understanding in the ' Alleluia ' office.

A very curious fact is that Borron was
evidently familiar with the tradition of the
Ritual Fish-Meal as observed by the early
Christian Church (cf. here Dr. Eisler's article
on ' The Messianic Fish-Meal of the Primitive
Church,' *The Quest*, vol. iv., No. 3), as is
proved by his story of Brons' capture of the
fish, of which no other Grail writer shows a
knowledge. Again, his account of Alain, his
pledge of virginity, and the fact that he
becomes the father of the Grail-Winner, is in
curious accord with the Nārada story of
world-origins, where the son of Brahma,

ordered by his father to wed and become the
progenitor of the human race, steadfastly
refuses, reproaching his father with being a
false teacher, yet is afterwards reckoned as
one of the Great Progenitors, and of all the
Indian sages the one whose teaching is of
most importance. A strange fact is that the
parallel extends to the absence in each case
of any reason for the change of mind; we
are never told why, and under what circumstances, Alain or Nārada reconsidered
their pledge of virginity. In fact, the more
closely we study Borron's version of the theme
the more we become impressed with the
nature and extent of his knowledge.

The position of the writer of the *Queste* is
less easy to determine. He certainly knew
the Grail to be the Source of Life, and
realized the fact that the end and aim of
such a Quest was, and could only be, the
attainment of conscious union with the
Divine. His version is written from the
Christian 'mystic' point of view—whether
he had any knowledge of the pre-Christian
' mystery ' tradition on which the story was
based is doubtful. It is true that he retains
the automatic, food-providing character of
the Grail, but he shows no knowledge of, or
care for, the traditional incidents of the story.
There is no abortive visit of the hero to the
Castle, no Grail procession, no Waste Land;
the personality of the lord of the Castle and

his relationship to the hero are very confused. The standpoint of the writer is that of the hagiographer rather than of a writer of chivalric romance. Galahad's feats are more reminiscent of the marvels wrought by a saint of *The Golden Legend* than of an initiate of the Greater Mysteries; the aim is spiritual indeed, but the method and presentation are crudely materialistic. The version of the *Queste* presupposes that of Borron, but the author is inferior in knowledge and breadth of conception.

The same criticism applies even more forcibly to the *Grand Saint Graal;* but here we are confronted with a curious element of heterodoxy. Josephe, the son of Joseph, consecrated by Christ Himself as first Bishop of His Church and Guardian of His Mysteries, is a figure quite impossible to reconcile with a loyal acceptance of the Petrine claims. If the writer of this romance really shared a Christian ' mystery ' tradition it was one which could not have been considered orthodox. He seems also to have had a considerable knowledge of sundry apocryphal *Acts*, on which he drew for his ' Conversion ' stories; the whole is a curious, and not specially edifying, composition.

The case of the *Parzival* is quite different. At first sight it might seem that the writer, Wolfram, or his source, had quite misunderstood his theme, but a closer knowledge of the subject shows that the case is far otherwise. With the exception of the first Grail author, Bleheris, and, as we have seen, probably also of Borron, no other writer betrays so thorough a knowledge of the real meaning of the story. He knows what is the real nature of the Grail King's disability, and he also knows that the result of the achievement of the Quest will be his restoration not only to health, but also to youth. He knows that the Grail is the Source of Life, and emphasizes that knowledge in a manner not to be found elsewhere. Thus of the inhabitants of the Grail Castle he says definitely, "*Sie lebent von einem steine*" (They live by a stone), and none who look upon it can die within seven days of that sight. If he chooses to show his 'occult' knowledge by replacing one form of the Life Quest by another, and representing the Grail not as a Vessel but as the Stone of the Alchemical Quest, that Stone is none the less 'The Grail.' If an additional argument for the correctness of the view which regards the Grail tradition as the record of a Quest for the Source of Life, be needed, it may surely be found in the fact that it explains, as no other theory has hitherto done, the peculiar character here assumed by the Talisman, and brings the poem naturally, and without any straining of evidence, within the cycle of Grail ideas and traditions.

That the mind responsible for the change in the outward presentment of the object of the Quest was the same which was responsible for the structure of the poem, the carefully designed historical connections, alike with the house of Anjou and the descendants of the mythical Swan-Knight,—that the peculiarity of the conception was the outcome of the learning which embraced a knowledge of Arabic lore and sidereal cults,—seems more than probable. But I do not for a moment believe that such learning was possessed by the simple Bavarian knight, Wolfram von Eschenbach, who proclaims emphatically that he knows nothing of the lore contained in books :

> *Swaz an den buochen stêt geschriben*
> *Des bin ich künstelôs beliben ;*

> (Of what stands written in books,
> Of that have I remained without skill ;)

and in another place :

> *i'ne kan decheinen buochstap.*

> (I know no letter.)

Who and what was the mysterious Kiot to whose authority he makes appeal, we do not, possibly we never shall, know, but there seems little doubt that we may reckon him among the small group of initiates who dealt, knowingly and understandingly, with their

great theme.   Of these I hold there were, to
our knowledge, three, who, each in his turn
from a different standpoint, but each with
equal understanding, handled the ' Secret of
the Grail.'

Bleheris knew the pre-Christian mystery
cult, its form and its intention, at the date
at which he lived, it may be, from tradition
only.

Borron knew the Christian ' mystery '
tradition, in its relation to the pre-Christian,
and understood perfectly how the symbolism
and terminology of the one could be translated into the symbolism and terminology of
the other.   The confusion which has arisen
in his version of the theme is due, not to any
lack of knowledge on his part, but, as I have
elsewhere shown, to the influence of a com-
peting and powerful interest, in the shape of
the Arthurian pseudo-historic tradition.

And if Borron knew the relation existing
between Christian and pre-Christian mystery
ritual, Kiot knew the relation between the
different forms of the Life-Quest, and how,
while changing the outward imagery, the
inward meaning could still be preserved
intact.   He knew how two objects, so apparently different from each other as the
Chalice of the Eucharist and a precious Stone,
could, in fact, represent precisely the same
idea, could both of them be ' The Grail.'   At
the same time there is in his version no trace

of the distinctively Christian ' mystic ' element, which, introduced by Borron, became so dominant in the *Queste*. If not heterodox, as is the *Grand Saint Graal*, the *Parzival* is far from being as militantly orthodox as are the *Queste* or the *Perlesvaus*; the poem, if marked by a genuine religious fervour, is also inspired by a wide tolerance. It is impossible not to feel that we are here dealing with an original and truly remarkable mind. I would submit that, with the Ritual theory for our guide, the apparent contradictions which mark the extant forms of our story resolve themselves into a general harmony of conception.

Nor does the acceptance of this theory involve the rejection of Christian and popular traditions as factors in the evolutionary process. As we have seen, the identification of the Grail in its lowest form with a Saint-Sang relic opened the way for the introduction of Nicodemus and Joseph of Arimathea, and the construction, with the aid of the pseudo-Gospel records, of an elaborate ' early-history ' of the relic. On the Folklore side, we may conjecture that certain peculiar features in the pre-Christian ritual feast encouraged the identification of the Grail, in its simplest, public form, with the automatic food-providing talisman of popular folk-tales. The introduction of such a feature as the mysterious disappearance of the Castle could be rationally accounted for—the aspirant, in a most probably artificially induced slumber, being conveyed to some distant point. But the very fact that it might happen, and therefore might well have formed part of the genuine tradition, would help to assimilate the tale to a folk-lore model, where such marvellous experiences were not uncommon. It is quite certain that, at a comparatively early stage of its evolution, the story of the Grail Quest became incorporated with a series of adventures of purely Folk-lore origin, the adventures of the hero we know as Perceval, and the combination thus formed was productive of admirable results, alike from the standpoint of literary form and of interpretation.

It may be well here to refer to the researches of an American scholar, Dr. Nitze, of Chicago University, as that critic, while adopting the theory of a Ritual origin for the story, has developed it upon lines differing from those indicated in this work. Thus Dr. Nitze would seek the origin of the story rather in the Eleusinian Mysteries than in the Adonis Cults. He believes the Grail story to be an integral part of the *Perceval* tradition, not an addition to that tale, and lays great stress on the relationship existing in this version between the hero and the Grail King.

Now it is undoubtedly true that, at a certain stage of social development, among certain, we may probably say the majority of peoples, the matriarchal system prevailed, and the sister's son was the due and rightful successor to his uncle. The father, whose identity was frequently doubtful, did not count. It is also quite true that this is a very marked feature of the *Perceval* story, where the identity of the father varies, and he is never the equal of the mother, always a princess, or queen in her own right; emphatically, ' a great lady.' It is also true that among many peoples great stress is laid on the rites attending the attainment of puberty and the admission of the youth into the full privileges of manhood, rites which often assume the character of an initiation.

On the other hand, it is by no means proved that the matriarchal principle was a feature of early Greek social organization ; it has, in fact, been strongly denied. Nor do we know that the priestly rights reserved to the two families, the Eumolpides and the Kerykes, who were responsible for the due celebration of the Eleusinian ritual, descended from uncle to nephew and were not equally enjoyed by all members of these clans. The fact that the inscription of a child as member of the family depended, as in other Athenian families, upon a declaration of paternity made on oath by the reputed father, seems to point strongly against the existence of mother-right. Nor do the Eleusinian Mysteries offer us the required *mise en scène.*

In my view the relationship of which Dr. Nitze makes so much, is to be regarded as a purely social, not in any sense a ritual, survival.   It is a lingering trace of the social conditions prevailing at the time when the *Perceval* story took form and shape, an interesting proof of the antiquity of the tale, *qua* tale.   At the same time it is a feature which is shared by other romantic traditions.   In all our romantic cycles the hero is the nephew of the ruling monarch, not his, but his sister's son.   This is the relation between Cuchullinn and Conchobar, between Diarmid and Finn, Gawain and Arthur, Roland and Charlemagne, Tristan and Mark ; and in this latter instance we have sufficient record of the Pictish rulers to lend support to the view that we are here dealing with a genuine historic tradition.   But in none of these cases is there the smallest trace of a ritual element, or signs of anything in the least resembling our Grail story.   In my view, the facts upon which Dr. Nitze relies in support of his theory that the Grail is an integral part of the *Perceval* story, are precisely facts which prove the contrary.

To my mind it is a significant point that while the Adonis ritual does provide us with the necessary sequence of incident and intention, none of the popular survivals, nor their striking correspondent parallels in Indian Vedic tradition, ever regard the 'medicine man,' whose *rôle* it is to restore to

life the representative of the Vegetation
Spirit, as in any way a relative; he is brought
in from the outside. Also, among those
peoples who have retained the primitive idea
of the dependence of the prosperity of the
folk, and of the fertility of the land, on the
health and vigour of the King, royalty is not
hereditary—facts which point rather to the
conclusion that versions in which the hero
is, as in the case of Gawain, no relation to the
Grail King, represent more accurately the
primitive form. In this connection certain
passages, both in the poems of Chrétien and
Wolfram and in other early Arthurian romances, which refer to Gawain's knowledge of
medicine and skill as physician, assume a
new significance. Such knowledge forms no
part of the ordinary chivalric equipment,
and hitherto it has been difficult to account
for its association with so purely romantic a
hero as Gawain. If, however, we admit that
Gawain was the original protagonist of the
Grail adventure, and that the source of that
adventure was as suggested in these pages,
then these passages assume an entirely different and important evidential character.

Thus, while admitting the value of much
of Dr. Nitze's work, and the light it has
thrown on certain features of the legend, I
cannot admit that the Eleusinian cult provides us with as satisfactory an explanation
of the peculiar features and incidents of the

Grail story as may be found in the more widely diffused Adonis ritual.

But it becomes more and more impossible to look upon the poem of Chrétien de Troyes as in any sense the starting-point of the story, more and more impossible to base upon the *données* of that poem any coherent theory of origins. There is no sign that Chrétien knew anything of the Grail in its 'mystery' aspect; he refers to it as '*sainte*'—"*tante sainte cose est li Greaus*" (so holy a thing is the Grail), a term which might well accord with his know-ledge of the talisman as a Saint-Sang relic, and as that alone; there is no evidence of a deeper knowledge. The interest of Chrétien's poem centres in the hero rather than in the quest, which in this special form is only one among many incidents, and really less im-portant than Gawain's adventures at the Chastel Merveilleus. As remarked above, the *Perceval* is a chivalric romance, not the record of a spiritual adventure. I have above referred to Dr. Nitze's work, and here it may be interesting to draw attention to his criticism of a point of detail which had escaped the attention of other scholars, but which may throw some light upon the source whence Chrétien's version was derived.

When the hero arrives at the Grail Castle he finds the host in the great hall, reclining on a couch before the fire which burns on a central hearth round which some four

hundred knights are seated.   In the *Parzival*
there are three such hearths round which the
couches for the knights are placed.   Now
Dr. Nitze has very acutely remarked that no
French hall of that date had a central fire-
place (by that time it had become the in-
variable practice to build the hearth against
the wall, generally at one end of the hall),
and that the description of the internal
arrangements of the Grail hall, the central
fires, and the seating of the knights correspond with remarkable fidelity to those prevailing in the famous hall of Tara, where the
outline of the hearths may still be traced.
Whether this arrangement of a central hearth
be genuinely Irish, or borrowed from the
Scandinavian during the period of the Viking
occupation (there is no doubt as to its use in
the North), is another matter ; what is quite
certain is that it is not French, and therefore
cannot be Chrétien's invention.

And if it is not easy to determine the nature
and source of Chrétien's knowledge, it is fully
as difficult to determine what his continuators
knew of the Grail.   All three alike, Wauchier,
Gerbert, and Manessier, drew from diverse
sources, and were at no pains to harmonize the very divergent statements.   Thus
Wauchier, while giving at full length the
Bleheris-*Gawain* visit, incorporates also a
version in which the Fisher King nightly
journeys abroad, accompanied by the Grail,

which gives light for his progress and preserves all who behold it from sin. This
version receives support from an interesting
passage in the unique *Merlin* MS. (B.N.
Fonds Franç. 337), where sundry knights of
Arthur's court meet a Grail procession in a
forest, the details of which correspond closely
with Wauchier's indications. Again, Wauchier
knows Perceval's sister, a maiden of saintly
life ; but Chrétien's hero has no sister. Thus
we may postulate on the part of Wauchier a
knowledge of at least three Grail versions :
one of which Gawain was the hero, one in
which Perceval had a sister (a form which
would approach that known to Borron, and
the author of the *Queste*), and Chrétien's
poem. The peripatetic Fisher King might
belong to the second form. Gerbert, again,
knew several (probably four) versions. Thus,
that which he designates as the ' *vraie
estoire* ' agrees with Wolfram, and may
very well preserve the source common to the
German and French poets, *i.e.* that used by
Kiot and Chrétien, but with features absent
from the latter and in some instances from
Wolfram. Other sections obviously derive
from a form of the *Perlesvaus* and the *Queste ;*
and he of course knows Chrétien. Manessier,
while he introduces his contribution to the
confused medley with a picturesque ' Ven-
geance ' tale which has no connection with
any other version of the story, concludes it in

a form showing strong affinity with Wolfram's version. None of these writers show themselves in the least disturbed by the manifold discrepancies in their presentation, or appear to possess such a definite and independent knowledge of their subject as would have enabled them to seize and co-ordinate the features of real significance. We must consider them, I think, as story-tellers, and as story-tellers only, and at the same time realize that the Grail romances which have descended to us form but a small portion of those which were current in the closing years of the twelfth and early years of the thirteenth centuries.

And then the fount of inspiration seems suddenly to have run dry ; as noted in the opening chapter, the sudden cessation of interest in the theme is as remarkable as its sudden popularity. Why, after those opening years of the thirteenth century, did no one write a Grail romance ? As noted above, they would not have lacked readers. May it not be that it was because the origin of the Grail was, as here suggested, not merely pre-Christian, but non-Christian, associated in its essence with ideas and practices which the Church, all-powerful in those days, could not countenance ? That even in its professedly Christian form it had passed through the medium, and bore the impress, of a body of thought and idea, which, known by the name of Gnosticism, was already under the Church's ban ?   That there were those among the ecclesiastical authorities who knew, quite as well as did Bleheris, Borron, or Kiot, what the Grail was, and whence it derived, and that such authorities steadily and silently discouraged the making of Grail romances ?

The *Parzival* suggests also the possible operation of other influences which would have a deterrent effect. There we find the Grail in the care of a body of semi-religious, semi-militant knights, who bear the significant name of Templeisen. Now one of the most interesting of unsolved historic problems is that connected with the fall of the Templars. No doubt their wealth excited the cupidity of the powers that be ; but what were the grounds on which it was possible to base an accusation of heresy sufficiently serious to bring about the destruction of so formidable and well-organized a body ? Were the Templars idolaters ? Were they Gnostics ? We cannot tell; but I am strongly inclined to believe that the connection between these knights and the Grail, indicated by the *Parzival* and hinted at by the *Perlesvaus* (where we have a body of knightly hermits, bearing the Cross on their robes), has a foundation in fact, and that the same influences which brought about the ruin of the one were responsible for the disappearance of the other.

The whole question of the later evolution of the Grail theme is surrounded by difficulties ; the steps of external Christianization are easily traced, but the precise conditions of thought and practice which made the Christianization from inside possible, which recognized alike the true character of the higher mystery teaching, and its relation to similar teaching within the limits of the Christian Faith, cannot be as readily determined. We know that the tradition of an esoteric doctrine persisted, and that, while in the West the tradition adjusted itself to Orthodox demands, and, assuming a contemplative and devotional character, lived on in the works of those Christian mystics whose writings we hold among our most precious treasures, and whose kinship with the pre-Christian philosophers Dr. Inge has demonstrated, in the East it retained more or less its original character. The home of this objective tradition, we are told, was mainly Byzantium, and the closer connection between East and West brought about by the Crusades may well have facilitated the infiltration of ideas and practices not indigenous to Western Christianity.

There is a stream of tradition, running as it were underground, which from time to time rises to the surface, only to be relentlessly suppressed. It may be the Troubadours, the symbolical language of whose love poems is held to convey another, and less innocent, meaning ; or the Albigenses, whose destruction the Church holds for a sacred duty. Alchemy, whose Elixir of Life and Philosopher's Stone are but names veiling a deeper and more spiritual meaning, belongs to the same family. I have myself seen an illustrated treatise on Alchemy, where the end sought is figured in a plate representing the Soul, crowned and enthroned, swallowing the Body. Of similar origin is that Free-Masonry which outside our own Islands is even to-day reckoned as the greatest enemy of the Christian Faith, and which still employs signs and symbols identical with those known and used in the Mysteries of long-vanished faiths.

Whatever may be the significance of these facts, we know, and every student of mediæval literature will bear the same witness, that there were strange currents stirring in those days, that more was believed, more was known, than the official guardians of faith and morals cared to admit, and that much, very much, of this undercurrent of yearning and investigation was concerned with the search for the source of Life—Life physical, Life immortal.

It is no empty claim we make when we contend that the Grail romances are a survival of that period of unrest, that they are to be treasured not merely as the remains, poor and fragmentary, of what must have been a great and enthralling body of literature, not merely as themselves literary monuments of no small value, as the works of Wolfram and Chrétien and Malory's noble renderings may well be reckoned, but as the record of a determined effort to attain, on the lower plane, to a definite and personal knowledge of the Secret of Life, on the higher, to that intimate and personal contact with the Divine Source of Life, in which, in the view of the mystics of all ages, is to be found the sole Reality.

It is from this point of view that the Search for the Grail is worthy of being reckoned among the great Quests, and of finding its place among the literature which deals with the deepest, and most keenly felt, of all human needs.

APPENDIX

THE GRAIL PROCESSION

THE following passages descriptive of the
various appearances of the Grail may enable
the reader to understand more clearly the
contradictory character of the evidence,
and the difficulty of finding a solution
which will harmonize such conflicting statements.

I give, in the original, French texts of which
no adequate translation has been published ;
where such translations are easily accessible
I cite these.

I begin with Chrétien de Troyes, as
his poem is still held by certain critics
to be the source of all the other existing
versions.

In Chrétien's description, as the hero sits
with the Fisher King and his knights in the
great hall of the Grail Castle, there enters a
youth, bearing a Lance of ' *fer blanc*,' from
the point of which a single drop of blood
runs down to the hand of the bearer ; then
two more with golden candlesticks, each

having, at least, ten lighted candles following
them :

> *Un graal entre ses II. mains*
> *Une damoisiele tenoit*
> *Qui avoec les varlés venoit*
> *Biele, gente, et acesmée.*
> *Quant ele fu laiens entrée*
> *Atout le graal qu'ele tint*
> *Une si grans clartés i vint*
> *Que si perdirent les candoiles*
> *Lor clarté com font les estoiles*
> *Quant li solaus lieve ou la lune.*
> *Apries içou en revint une*
> *Qui tint le tailléor d'argent.*
> *Içou vos di veraiement*
> *De fin or esmerée estoit,*
> *Piéres pressieuses avoit*
> *El graal de maintes manières,*
> *Des plus rices et des plus cieres*
> *Qui el mont ou en tiere soient,*
> *Totes autres pieres passoient*
> *Celes du greal sans dotance.*
>
> (Potvin, ll. 4398–417.)

> (A grail between her two hands
> A maiden held,
> Who with the squires came,
> Fair, gracious, and richly clad.
> When she had entered therein
> With the grail she held,
> So great a light came there
> That the candles lost
> Their light as do the stars
> When sun or moon ariseth.
> After this maiden came one
> Who bare the *tailléor* of silver;
> I tell ye verily,
> Of pure refined gold it was,
> And precious stones it had,

The grail, of many kinds,
The richest and most precious
That were in the world or on earth ;
All other stones were surpassed
By those of the grail, without doubt.)

The version of Wolfram von Eschenbach
is much more detailed ; the squire holding
the Lance from which the blood ran fast
" adown to the hand of the holder till 'twas
lost in his sleeve at last," makes the circuit
of the hall and disappears before there is any
sign of the Grail procession.   When it enters
it is ordered on this wise :

At the end of the hall a doorway of steel did they
    open fair
And two noble children entered.   Now hearken what
    guise they bare
An a knight for love would serve them, with love
    they his task might pay,
For such fair and gracious maidens as e'er man
    might woo were they.
Each wore on her hair loose flowing a chaplet of
    blossoms, bound
With a silken band, beneath it, their tresses, they
    sought the ground.
And the hand of each maiden carried a candlestick
    all of gold,
And every golden socket did a burning taper hold.
Nor would I forget the raiment these gentle maidens
    ware,
For one was Tenabroc's countess, ruddy brown was
    her robe so fair,
And the selfsame garb wore the maiden who beside
    the countess paced,
And with girdles rich and costly were they girt
    round each slender waist.

And behind them there came a duchess and her
fellow ; of ivory white
Two stools they bare, and glowing their lips, e'en as
fire is bright.
Then they bowed, the four, and bending, the stools
'fore the host they laid,
Nor was aught to their service lacking, but fitly their
part they played.
Then they stood, all four together, and their faces
were fair to see,
And the vesture of each fair maiden was like to the
other three.

Now see how they followed swiftly, fair maidens
twice told four,
And this was, I ween, their office, four tapers tall
they bore,
Nor the others deemed too heavy the weight of a
precious stone,
And by day the sun shone thro' it, as Jacinth its
name is known.
'Twas long and broad, and for lightness had they
fashioned it fair and meet,
To serve at will for a table where a wealthy host
might eat.
And straight to the host they stepped them, and
they bowed their fair heads low,
And four laid the costly table on the ivory white as snow,
The stools they had placed aforetime—then, courteous,
they turned aside,
And there by their four companions stood the eight
in their maiden pride.
And green were the robes of these maidens, green
as grass in the month of May,
Of samite, in Assagog woven, both long and wide
were they,
And girt at the waist with a girdle, narrow, and
long, and fair,
And each of these gentle maidens wore a wreath on
her shining hair.

Now Iwân, the Count of Nonel, and Jernis, the Lord
    of Reil,
To the Grail were their daughters summoned, from
    many a distant mile,
And they came, these two princesses, in raiment
    wondrous fair,
And two keen-edged knives, a marvel, on cloths did
    those maidens bear.
Of silver white and shining were they wrought, with
    such cunning skill
So sharp, that methinks their edges e'en steel might
    they cut at will.
And maidens four went before them, for this should
    their office be,
To bear tapers before the silver, four children from
    falsehood free.
Six maidens all told, they entered, and took thro'
    the hall their way,
Now hearken, and I will tell ye the service they did
    that day.
They bowed, and the twain who carried the silver,
    they laid it low
On the Jacinth, and courteous turning, to the twelve
    in order go.
And now, have I counted rightly, here shall eighteen
    maidens stand,
And lo! six again come hither in vesture from
    distant land,
Half of silk with gold thread inwoven, half of silk
    of Nineveh bright,
For they, and the six before them, parti-coloured
    their robes of light.

And last of those maids a maiden, o'er the others
    was she queen,
So fair her face that they thought them 'twas the
    morning's dawn, I ween!
And they saw her clad in raiment of pfellel of
    Araby,
And she bare aloft on a cushion of verdant Achmârdi,

Root and blossom of Paradise garden, that thing
    which men call *The Grail*,
The crown of all earthly wishes, fair fulness that
    ne'er shall fail!
Repanse de Schoie did they call her, in whose hands
    the Grail might lie,
By the Grail Itself elected was she to this office high.
And they who would here do service, those maids
    must be pure of heart,
And true in life, nor falsehood shall have in their
    dealings part.

And lights both rare and costly before the Grail
    they bore,
Six glasses tall, transparent, and wondrous balsam's
    store
Burst therein with a strange sweet perfume; with
    measured steps they came,
And the queen bowed low with the maidens who
    bare the balsam's flame.
And this maiden, free from falsehood, the Grail on
    the Jacinth laid;
And Parzival looked upon her, beholding the royal
    maid
Elect to so high an office, whose mantle he needs
    must wear.
Then the seven, courteous, turned them to the
    eighteen maidens fair,
And the noblest they placed in the centre, and
    twelve on either side,
They stood, but the crownèd maiden, no beauty with
    her's had vied!

(Parzival, Book v. ll. 137–204.)

No other text gives a Grail procession to
compare with this in stately dignity. Later
on (Book ix.), we are told that the mysterious
object is the Stone, ' *Lapis Exilis*,' by virtue
of which the Phœnix renews its youth ; none

can die within eight days of beholding it, and those who live in its service rejoice in perpetual youth : " Young they abide for ever, and this Stone all men call *The Grail* " (ix. ll. 626–40).

In the prose *Perceval* we read :

" *Ensi com il seoient, et on lor aportoit le premier més, si virent d'une cambre issir une damiesele molt ricement atirée, et avoit une touaile entor son col, et portoit en ses mains II. tailléors d'argent. Après vint uns valles qui aporta une lance, et sainoit par le fer III. gouttes de sanc, et entroient en une cambre par devant Perceval, et après si vint uns valles, et portoit entre ses mains le vaissel que Nostre Sire douna a Joseph en le prison, et le porta molt hautement entre ses mains ; et quant li sire le vit si l'enclina, et rendi se cope, et tot cil de l'ostel autresi* " (Modena MS., p. 59).

(As they sat thus, and were served with the first meat, they saw issue from a chamber a maiden, very richly clad, with a towel round her neck, and she bare in her hands two little *tailléors* of silver ; after her came a squire, who bare a lance the blade of which bled three drops of blood ; and they entered a chamber opposite to Perceval. And after came a squire, who bare between his hands the Vessel which Our Lord gave to Joseph in the prison, and he bare it on high, betwixt his hands, and when the lord saw it he bowed towards it, and beat his breast, and all those of the hostel did the like.)

It may be worth noting here that the *tailléors* which figure in some versions of the procession are a veritable *crux* for the critic. The word really means a platter on which meat is carved, and what such an object can have to do with the Grail is not very clear. It will be noted that Wolfram instead of two silver *tailléors* has two silver knives, a point which has been seized upon by the advocates of the dependence of the German upon the French poem, as a proof that he was following, and misunderstanding, Chrétien's version. He knew the word had some connection with cutting, and translated *tailléor* as ' knife.' (It may be noted that while Chrétien has *one tailléor*, Wolfram has *two* knives.) But as a matter of fact, it is easier to account for the presence of two knives in the Grail procession, than for that of one, or two, platters. The Fescamp ' Saint-Sang ' relic had its double in the knife with which Nicodemus cleansed the dried blood from the wounds of the Redeemer; the two were preserved together at Fescamp. A second knife was mysteriously brought thither and deposited upon the altar, during the dedication service, by an angel in the garb of a pilgrim. If, as I have suggested above, the original home of the Christian Grail tradition was Fescamp, the two knives connected with that Abbey may well have figured in the earlier versions.

In the *Perlesvaus* the abortive visit of the hero precedes the opening of the story, and the proccession is witnessed by Gawain :

" Thereon, lo, you, two damsels that issue forth of a chapel, whereof the one holdeth in her hands the most Holy Grail, and the other the Lance whereof the point bleedeth thereinto.   And the one goeth beside the other in the midst of the hall where the knights and Messire Gawain sat at meat, and so sweet a smell, and so holy, came to them therefrom that they forgat to eat.   Messire Gawain looketh at the Grail, and it seemed to him that a chalice was therein, albeit none there was as at this time, and he seeth the point of the Lance whence the red blood ran thereinto, and it seemeth to him that he seeth two angels, that bear two candlesticks of gold, filled with candles.   And the damsels pass before Messire Gawain, and go into another chapel " (*High History of the Holy Grail*, vol. i. branch vi. chap. xix.).

In *Diu Crône*, where Gawain is again the witness, we read :

" At the last came, in fair procession as it were, four seneschals, and as the last passed the door was the palace filled—nor were it fitting that I say more. In the sight of all there paced into the hall two maidens fair and graceful, bearing two candlesticks ; behind each maid there came a youth, and the twain held between them a sharp spear. After these came other two maidens, fair in form, and richly clad, who bare a salver of gold and precious stones upon a silken cloth, and behind them, treading soft and slow, paced the fairest being whom since the world began God had wrought in woman's wise, perfect was she in form and feature, and richly clad withal. Before her she held on a rich cloth of samite a jewel wrought of red gold, in form of a base, whereon there stood another, of gold and gems, fashioned even as a reliquary that standeth upon an altar. This maiden bare upon her head a crown of gold, and behind her came another, wondrous fair, who wept and made lament, but the others spake never a word, only drew nigh unto the host, and bowed them low before him " (*Sir Gawain at the Grail Castle*, p. 40).

The Spear is laid upon the table and sheds three drops of blood into the salver placed beneath it.

In the prose *Lancelot* there is a solemn entry' of the Grail, but the procession is lacking. A white dove, with a golden censer in its beak, enters by the open window and passes through the hall into a chamber ; the palace is filled with sweetest odours, and the folk, without speaking a word, prepare the tables, and sit down, 'in prayers and orisons.'

" With that there came forth from the chamber wherein the dove had entered a damsel, the fairest he (Sir Gawain) had beheld any day of his life, and without fail was she the fairest maiden then alive, nor was her peer thereafter born. Her hair was cunningly plaited, and her face was fair to look upon. She was beautiful with all the beauty that pertaineth unto a woman, none fairer was ever seen on earth. She came forth from the chamber bearing in her hands the richest vessel that might be beheld by the eye of mortal man. 'Twas made in the semblance of a chalice, and she held it on high above her head, so that she ever bowed before it " (*Sir Gawain at the Grail Castle*, p. 55).

(Then follows the passage cited above, p. 2, as to the mysterious nature of the Vessel.)

Certain of the *Perceval* MSS. contain a visit of Gawain to the castle, previous to that derived from Bleheris, and distinguished by a Grail procession, the details of which agree now with the *Perceval* now with the *Gawain* tradition. It runs as follows :

As they sit at meat a very fair youth enters, bearing a Lance which bleeds ceaselessly,

> *Et le fer de la lance saine*
> *Ainz de saignier ne se lassa.*

He passed through the hall, and then Gawain sees :

D'une chambre issir parmi l'uis
Une pucele belle et gente ;
En li esgarder mist s'entente
Gauvains, et durement li plot ;
Et la pucele si portot
I. petit tailléor d'argent,
Par devant trestote la gent
S'en passa outre après la lance.
Après ce revit sans doutance,
II. vallez Mesire Gauvains
Qui portoit chandeliers plains
De chandelles toutes ardanz,
Moult estoit engrès et ardanz
Mesire Gauvains de l'enquerre
Quel gent se sont, et de quel terre ;
Quanque Gauvains ainsi pensoit,
Après les vallez venir voit
Parmi la sale une pucele
Qui moult estoit et gente et bele,
Mès moult plore et se desconforte ;
Entre ses mains hautement porte
I. graal trestout descovert.
Gauvains le vit tout en apert,
Si s'en merveille durement,
Por qu'ele plore si forment,
Et ou ele va, et qu'ele porte.
De ce qu'ele ne se conforte,
Et que de plorer ne se lasse,
Se merveille, et cele s'en passe
Par devant eux grant aléure,
En une chambre entre à droiture,
Et, quant ele fu ens entrée
IIII. valles ont aportée
Une bière après le Graal
Couverte d'un paile roial ;
Si ot dedenz la bière I. cors
Et sor le paile par defors

Avoit une espée couchiée
Qui par milieu estoit brisiée.
 (MS. Montpellier, printed by Potvin at end
  of vol. iii. of his edition of Chrétien's
  poem.)

This procession passes and repasses three
times. Then Gawain sees :

Issue from the door of a chamber,
A maiden fair and gracious ;
He set his mind to gaze upon her,
Gawain, and greatly she pleased him.
And the maiden bare
A little *tailléor* of silver,
And before all the folk
She passed on after the Lance.
After that he saw again without doubt,
Sir Gawain, two squires
Who bare candlesticks full
Of candles all burning,
Very keen and eager
Was Sir Gawain to ask
Who were this folk, and of what land ?
And as Gawain mused thus,
Following the squires, he saw come
Thro' the hall, a maiden
Who was very gracious and fair ;
But much she wept, and discomforted herself.
Between her hands she bare aloft
A Grail, all uncovered.
Gawain beheld it openly,
And greatly he marvelled
Why she wept thus sorely,
And whither she went, and what she bare.
Of this, that she was not comforted,
And stayed not her weeping,
He marvelled. And she passed
Before them swiftly,
Entering straightway into a chamber.

And when she was thither entered,
Four squires have borne
A bier after the Grail
Covered with a royal pall;
Within the bier was a body,
And without, on the silk,
There lay a sword
Which was broken in the middle.

In the curious unpublished *Merlin* MS., B.N. 337, certain knights of the Round Table meet the Grail procession passing through a forest; here it is composed of a white stag, with a red cross on the forehead and lighted tapers on the horns, carrying on its back a Vessel, beneath a rich silken covering, and followed by a white brachet, and a little maiden leading in a leash two small white beasts, the size of rabbits. The procession is closed by a knight in a litter borne by four little palefrois, while voices in the air above are heard singing: "Honour, and glory, and power, and everlasting joy to the Destroyer of Death!" I have suggested above (p. 134) that the version from which this description was derived may have been known to Wauchier.

In the *Bleheris* and *Queste* versions, the Grail, as we have seen, is automatic, and requires no Bearer.

BIBLIOGRAPHY

Perceval or *Le Conte du Graal.* CHRÉTIEN DE
TROYES. Ed. CH. POTVIN (*Société des Biblio-
philes de Mons*), 6 vols., 1886–71.
    Out of print and difficult to procure. The
MS. of Mons represents a very inferior text, and
Potvin frequently misread his original, but it
comprises both the Wauchier and Manessier
continuations, and the editor has added an
abstract of the Gerbert text. An edition of
the *Perceval* MS. B.N. F. Fr. 794, to the end
of Chrétien's poem, has been published by
Professor Baist, for private circulation only.
Miss Mary Williams and M. Mario Roques are
preparing an edition of the Gerbert continuation from MS. B N. F. Fr. 12576, the best
Perceval text, for publication in *Les Classiques
Français du Moyen Age*, and it is to be hoped
that the entire text will follow. A complete
and reliable edition of Chrétien's poem is
greatly needed.

Perlesvaus.—The French text is contained in vol i.
of POTVIN's edition. An English translation
by Dr. SEBASTIAN EVANS is published in
' The Temple Classics,' under the title of *The
High History of the Holy Grail.*
    From a literary point of view Dr. Evans'
rendering is a fine piece of work, but he had

little knowledge of the literature of the cycle, and his views as to the origin of the Grail story, the position of the romance in the cycle, and its critical value as an authority, are frankly absurd. His theory of the origin of the story, in especial, is an extreme instance of the fan-tastic ingenuity which has been lavished on the problem. A critical edition of the *Perles-vaus* is being prepared by Dr. Nitze.

Parzival, WOLFRAM VON ESCHENBACH.—This poem has been several times edited. The most accessible text is that by Bartsch, in *Deutsche Classiker des Mittelalters.* There are critical editions by Lachmann, and Martin. It has been translated into modern German by K. Simrock, and by W. Hertz. Simrock's version is the closest to the original text, but Hertz was a real poet and a scholar of wide reading, and his translation, with Notes and Appendices, is a very useful and valuable work.

An English translation, by J. L. Weston, *Parzival, A Knightly Epic,* was published by Nutt in 1894. The *Parzival* is the only romance of the entire cycle which has been critically edited.

The prose *Perceval,* or ' Didot ' *Perceval,* was published by Hucher in vol. i. of his edition of *Le Grand Saint Graal* (*Le Saint Graal,* 3 vols., 1874), from the Firmin-Didot MS. The *Joseph of Arimathea* will be found in the same edition. The much superior Modena MS. was published by J. L. Weston, in vol. ii. of *The Legend of Sir Perceval* (Nutt, 1906). Both texts obviously derive from a common, and much fuller, original.

The *Queste* was published by Dr. Furnivall for the

Roxburghe Club in 1864, and there has been
no later edition. This is of less importance,
however, as Malory's translation gives the
romance practically *in extenso*. It occupies
Books xiii. to xvii., inclusive, of the *Morte
Arthure*.

Diu Crône was edited by Scholl, in 1852. The
book is out of print and difficult to obtain.

Sir Gawain at the Grail Castle (*Arthurian Romances*,
vi., Nutt, 1903) includes the Bleheris-*Gawain*
version, that of *Diu Crône*, and that of the
prose *Lancelot*, translated from the original
texts by J. L. Weston.

For a general survey of the literature, the books
mentioned in Chapter II., *Die Sage vom Gral*,
Birch-Hirschfeld, and *Studies in the Legend of
the Holy Grail*, Alfred Nutt, are to be recommended, as they include lengthy abstracts of
the various texts. The last-named writer's
little brochure, *The Holy Grail*, in *Popular
Studies on Romance and Folk-Lore* (Nutt), is of
later date, and gives a very useful summary.
Those who desire a more exact knowledge
should consult *The Legend of Sir Perceval*,
J. L. Weston, 'Grimm Library,' vols. xvii. and
xix. (Nutt). Vol. i. contains an analysis of the
versions of Chrétien and Wauchier, with a
detailed description and classification of the
MSS. of the poem. Vol. ii. contains the Modena
prose text, and a study on the development of
the Grail Legend, with a table showing the
probable relation between the different versions. There is also a bibliography, giving not
only the editions of the texts, but the principal
studies devoted to their elucidation.

INDEX

A CATALOG OF SELECTED
DOVER BOOKS
IN ALL FIELDS OF INTEREST

A CATALOG OF SELECTED DOVER
BOOKS IN ALL FIELDS OF INTEREST

CONCERNING THE SPIRITUAL IN ART, Wassily Kandinsky. Pioneering work by father of abstract art. Thoughts on color theory, nature of art. Analysis of earlier masters. 12 illustrations. 80pp. of text. 5⅜ x 8½. 23411-8 Pa. $4.95

ANIMALS: 1,419 Copyright-Free Illustrations of Mammals, Birds, Fish, Insects, etc., Jim Harter (ed.). Clear wood engravings present, in extremely lifelike poses, over 1,000 species of animals. One of the most extensive pictorial sourcebooks of its kind. Captions. Index. 284pp. 9 x 12. 23766-4 Pa. $14.95

CELTIC ART: The Methods of Construction, George Bain. Simple geometric techniques for making Celtic interlacements, spirals, Kells-type initials, animals, humans, etc. Over 500 illustrations. 160pp. 9 x 12. (Available in U.S. only.) 22923-8 Pa. $9.95

AN ATLAS OF ANATOMY FOR ARTISTS, Fritz Schider. Most thorough reference work on art anatomy in the world. Hundreds of illustrations, including selections from works by Vesalius, Leonardo, Goya, Ingres, Michelangelo, others. 593 illustrations. 192pp. 7⅛ x 10¼. 20241-0 Pa. $9.95

CELTIC HAND STROKE-BY-STROKE (Irish Half-Uncial from "The Book of Kells"): An Arthur Baker Calligraphy Manual, Arthur Baker. Complete guide to creating each letter of the alphabet in distinctive Celtic manner. Covers hand position, strokes, pens, inks, paper, more. Illustrated. 48pp. 8¼ x 11. 24336-2 Pa. $3.95

EASY ORIGAMI, John Montroll. Charming collection of 32 projects (hat, cup, pelican, piano, swan, many more) specially designed for the novice origami hobbyist. Clearly illustrated easy-to-follow instructions insure that even beginning papercrafters will achieve successful results. 48pp. 8¼ x 11. 27298-2 Pa. $3.50

THE COMPLETE BOOK OF BIRDHOUSE CONSTRUCTION FOR WOODWORKERS, Scott D. Campbell. Detailed instructions, illustrations, tables. Also data on bird habitat and instinct patterns. Bibliography. 3 tables. 63 illustrations in 15 figures. 48pp. 5¼ x 8½. 24407-5 Pa. $2.50

BLOOMINGDALE'S ILLUSTRATED 1886 CATALOG: Fashions, Dry Goods and Housewares, Bloomingdale Brothers. Famed merchants' extremely rare catalog depicting about 1,700 products: clothing, housewares, firearms, dry goods, jewelry, more. Invaluable for dating, identifying vintage items. Also, copyright-free graphics for artists, designers. Co-published with Henry Ford Museum & Greenfield Village. 160pp. 8¼ x 11. 25780-0 Pa. $12.95

HISTORIC COSTUME IN PICTURES, Braun & Schneider. Over 1,450 costumed figures in clearly detailed engravings–from dawn of civilization to end of 19th century. Captions. Many folk costumes. 256pp. 8⅜ x 11¾. 23150-X Pa. $12.95

STICKLEY CRAFTSMAN FURNITURE CATALOGS, Gustav Stickley and L. & J. G. Stickley. Beautiful, functional furniture in two authentic catalogs from 1910. 594 illustrations, including 277 photos, show settles, rockers, armchairs, reclining chairs, bookcases, desks, tables. 183pp. 6½ x 9¼.   23838-5 Pa. $11.95

AMERICAN LOCOMOTIVES IN HISTORIC PHOTOGRAPHS: 1858 to 1949, Ron Ziel (ed.). A rare collection of 126 meticulously detailed official photographs, called "builder portraits," of American locomotives that majestically chronicle the rise of steam locomotive power in America. Introduction. Detailed captions. xi+129pp. 9 x 12.   27393-8 Pa. $13.95

AMERICA'S LIGHTHOUSES: An Illustrated History, Francis Ross Holland, Jr. Delightfully written, profusely illustrated fact-filled survey of over 200 American lighthouses since 1716. History, anecdotes, technological advances, more. 240pp. 8 x 10¾.
                                                                          25576-X Pa. $12.95

TOWARDS A NEW ARCHITECTURE, Le Corbusier. Pioneering manifesto by founder of "International School." Technical and aesthetic theories, views of industry, economics, relation of form to function, "mass-production split" and much more. Profusely illustrated. 320pp. 6⅛ x 9¼. (Available in U.S. only.)   25023-7 Pa. $10.95

HOW THE OTHER HALF LIVES, Jacob Riis. Famous journalistic record, exposing poverty and degradation of New York slums around 1900, by major social reformer. 100 striking and influential photographs. 233pp. 10 x 7⅞.
                                                                          22012-5 Pa. $11.95

FRUIT KEY AND TWIG KEY TO TREES AND SHRUBS, William M. Harlow. One of the handiest and most widely used identification aids. Fruit key covers 120 deciduous and evergreen species; twig key 160 deciduous species. Easily used. Over 300 photographs. 126pp. 5⅜ x 8½.   20511-8 Pa. $3.95

COMMON BIRD SONGS, Dr. Donald J. Borror. Songs of 60 most common U.S. birds: robins, sparrows, cardinals, bluejays, finches, more–arranged in order of increasing complexity. Up to 9 variations of songs of each species.
                                                       Cassette and manual 99911-4 $8.95

ORCHIDS AS HOUSE PLANTS, Rebecca Tyson Northen. Grow cattleyas and many other kinds of orchids–in a window, in a case, or under artificial light. 63 illustrations. 148pp. 5⅜ x 8½.   23261-1 Pa. $7.95

MONSTER MAZES, Dave Phillips. Masterful mazes at four levels of difficulty. Avoid deadly perils and evil creatures to find magical treasures. Solutions for all 32 exciting illustrated puzzles. 48pp. 8¼ x 11.   26005-4 Pa. $2.95

MOZART'S DON GIOVANNI (DOVER OPERA LIBRETTO SERIES), Wolfgang Amadeus Mozart. Introduced and translated by Ellen H. Bleiler. Standard Italian libretto, with complete English translation. Convenient and thoroughly portable–an ideal companion for reading along with a recording or the performance itself. Introduction. List of characters. Plot summary. 121pp. 5¼ x 8½.
                                                                          24944-1 Pa. $3.95

TECHNICAL MANUAL AND DICTIONARY OF CLASSICAL BALLET, Gail Grant. Defines, explains, comments on steps, movements, poses and concepts. 15-page pictorial section. Basic book for student, viewer. 127pp. 5⅜ x 8½.
                                                                          21843-0 Pa. $4.95

THE CLARINET AND CLARINET PLAYING, David Pino. Lively, comprehensive work features suggestions about technique, musicianship, and musical interpretation, as well as guidelines for teaching, making your own reeds, and preparing for public performance. Includes an intriguing look at clarinet history. "A godsend," *The Clarinet,* Journal of the International Clarinet Society. Appendixes. 7 illus. 320pp. 5⅜ x 8½. 40270-3 Pa. $9.95

HOLLYWOOD GLAMOR PORTRAITS, John Kobal (ed.). 145 photos from 1926-49. Harlow, Gable, Bogart, Bacall; 94 stars in all. Full background on photographers, technical aspects. 160pp. 8⅜ x 11¼. 23352-9 Pa. $12.95

THE ANNOTATED CASEY AT THE BAT: A Collection of Ballads about the Mighty Casey/Third, Revised Edition, Martin Gardner (ed.). Amusing sequels and parodies of one of America's best-loved poems: Casey's Revenge, Why Casey Whiffed, Casey's Sister at the Bat, others. 256pp. 5⅜ x 8½. 28598-7 Pa. $8.95

THE RAVEN AND OTHER FAVORITE POEMS, Edgar Allan Poe. Over 40 of the author's most memorable poems: "The Bells," "Ulalume," "Israfel," "To Helen," "The Conqueror Worm," "Eldorado," "Annabel Lee," many more. Alphabetic lists of titles and first lines. 64pp. 5³⁄₁₆ x 8¼. 26685-0 Pa. $1.00

PERSONAL MEMOIRS OF U. S. GRANT, Ulysses Simpson Grant. Intelligent, deeply moving firsthand account of Civil War campaigns, considered by many the finest military memoirs ever written. Includes letters, historic photographs, maps and more. 528pp. 6⅛ x 9¼. 28587-1 Pa. $12.95

ANCIENT EGYPTIAN MATERIALS AND INDUSTRIES, A. Lucas and J. Harris. Fascinating, comprehensive, thoroughly documented text describes this ancient civilization's vast resources and the processes that incorporated them in daily life, including the use of animal products, building materials, cosmetics, perfumes and incense, fibers, glazed ware, glass and its manufacture, materials used in the mummification process, and much more. 544pp. 6⅛ x 9¼. (Available in U.S. only.) 40446-3 Pa. $16.95

RUSSIAN STORIES/PYCCKNE PACCKA3bl: A Dual-Language Book, edited by Gleb Struve. Twelve tales by such masters as Chekhov, Tolstoy, Dostoevsky, Pushkin, others. Excellent word-for-word English translations on facing pages, plus teaching and study aids, Russian/English vocabulary, biographical/critical introductions, more. 416pp. 5⅜ x 8½. 26244-8 Pa. $9.95

PHILADELPHIA THEN AND NOW: 60 Sites Photographed in the Past and Present, Kenneth Finkel and Susan Oyama. Rare photographs of City Hall, Logan Square, Independence Hall, Betsy Ross House, other landmarks juxtaposed with contemporary views. Captures changing face of historic city. Introduction. Captions. 128pp. 8¼ x 11. 25790-8 Pa. $9.95

AIA ARCHITECTURAL GUIDE TO NASSAU AND SUFFOLK COUNTIES, LONG ISLAND, The American Institute of Architects, Long Island Chapter, and the Society for the Preservation of Long Island Antiquities. Comprehensive, well-researched and generously illustrated volume brings to life over three centuries of Long Island's great architectural heritage. More than 240 photographs with authoritative, extensively detailed captions. 176pp. 8¼ x 11. 26946-9 Pa. $14.95

NORTH AMERICAN INDIAN LIFE: Customs and Traditions of 23 Tribes, Elsie Clews Parsons (ed.). 27 fictionalized essays by noted anthropologists examine religion, customs, government, additional facets of life among the Winnebago, Crow, Zuni, Eskimo, other tribes. 480pp. 6⅛ x 9¼. 27377-6 Pa. $10.95

FRANK LLOYD WRIGHT'S DANA HOUSE, Donald Hoffmann. Pictorial essay of residential masterpiece with over 160 interior and exterior photos, plans, elevations, sketches and studies. 128pp. 9¼ x 10¾. 29120-0 Pa. $14.95

THE MALE AND FEMALE FIGURE IN MOTION: 60 Classic Photographic Sequences, Eadweard Muybridge. 60 true-action photographs of men and women walking, running, climbing, bending, turning, etc., reproduced from rare 19th-century masterpiece. vi + 121pp. 9 x 12. 24745-7 Pa. $12.95

1001 QUESTIONS ANSWERED ABOUT THE SEASHORE, N. J. Berrill and Jacquelyn Berrill. Queries answered about dolphins, sea snails, sponges, starfish, fishes, shore birds, many others. Covers appearance, breeding, growth, feeding, much more. 305pp. 5¼ x 8¼. 23366-9 Pa. $9.95

ATTRACTING BIRDS TO YOUR YARD, William J. Weber. Easy-to-follow guide offers advice on how to attract the greatest diversity of birds: birdhouses, feeders, water and waterers, much more. 96pp. 5³⁄₁₆ x 8¼. 28927-3 Pa. $2.50

MEDICINAL AND OTHER USES OF NORTH AMERICAN PLANTS: A Historical Survey with Special Reference to the Eastern Indian Tribes, Charlotte Erichsen-Brown. Chronological historical citations document 500 years of usage of plants, trees, shrubs native to eastern Canada, northeastern U.S. Also complete identifying information. 343 illustrations. 544pp. 6½ x 9¼. 25951-X Pa. $12.95

STORYBOOK MAZES, Dave Phillips. 23 stories and mazes on two-page spreads: Wizard of Oz, Treasure Island, Robin Hood, etc. Solutions. 64pp. 8¼ x 11. 23628-5 Pa. $2.95

AMERICAN NEGRO SONGS: 230 Folk Songs and Spirituals, Religious and Secular, John W. Work. This authoritative study traces the African influences of songs sung and played by black Americans at work, in church, and as entertainment. The author discusses the lyric significance of such songs as "Swing Low, Sweet Chariot," "John Henry," and others and offers the words and music for 230 songs. Bibliography. Index of Song Titles. 272pp. 6½ x 9¼. 40271-1 Pa. $10.95

MOVIE-STAR PORTRAITS OF THE FORTIES, John Kobal (ed.). 163 glamor, studio photos of 106 stars of the 1940s: Rita Hayworth, Ava Gardner, Marlon Brando, Clark Gable, many more. 176pp. 8⅜ x 11¼. 23546-7 Pa. $14.95

BENCHLEY LOST AND FOUND, Robert Benchley. Finest humor from early 30s, about pet peeves, child psychologists, post office and others. Mostly unavailable elsewhere. 73 illustrations by Peter Arno and others. 183pp. 5⅜ x 8½. 22410-4 Pa. $6.95

YEKL and THE IMPORTED BRIDEGROOM AND OTHER STORIES OF YIDDISH NEW YORK, Abraham Cahan. Film Hester Street based on *Yekl* (1896). Novel, other stories among first about Jewish immigrants on N.Y.'s East Side. 240pp. 5⅜ x 8½. 22427-9 Pa. $7.95

SELECTED POEMS, Walt Whitman. Generous sampling from *Leaves of Grass*. Twenty-four poems include "I Hear America Singing," "Song of the Open Road," "I Sing the Body Electric," "When Lilacs Last in the Dooryard Bloom'd," "O Captain! My Captain!"–all reprinted from an authoritative edition. Lists of titles and first lines. 128pp. 5³⁄₁₆ x 8¼. 26878-0 Pa. $1.00

THE BEST TALES OF HOFFMANN, E. T. A. Hoffmann. 10 of Hoffmann's most important stories: "Nutcracker and the King of Mice," "The Golden Flowerpot," etc. 458pp. 5⅜ x 8½. 21793-0 Pa. $9.95

FROM FETISH TO GOD IN ANCIENT EGYPT, E. A. Wallis Budge. Rich detailed survey of Egyptian conception of "God" and gods, magic, cult of animals, Osiris, more. Also, superb English translations of hymns and legends. 240 illustrations. 545pp. 5⅜ x 8½. 25803-3 Pa. $13.95

FRENCH STORIES/CONTES FRANÇAIS: A Dual-Language Book, Wallace Fowlie. Ten stories by French masters, Voltaire to Camus: "Micromegas" by Voltaire; "The Atheist's Mass" by Balzac; "Minuet" by de Maupassant; "The Guest" by Camus, six more. Excellent English translations on facing pages. Also French-English vocabulary list, exercises, more. 352pp. 5⅜ x 8½. 26443-2 Pa. $9.95

CHICAGO AT THE TURN OF THE CENTURY IN PHOTOGRAPHS: 122 Historic Views from the Collections of the Chicago Historical Society, Larry A. Viskochil. Rare large-format prints offer detailed views of City Hall, State Street, the Loop, Hull House, Union Station, many other landmarks, circa 1904-1913. Introduction. Captions. Maps. 144pp. 9⅜ x 12¼. 24656-6 Pa. $12.95

OLD BROOKLYN IN EARLY PHOTOGRAPHS, 1865-1929, William Lee Younger. Luna Park, Gravesend race track, construction of Grand Army Plaza, moving of Hotel Brighton, etc. 157 previously unpublished photographs. 165pp. 8⅞ x 11¾. 23587-4 Pa. $13.95

THE MYTHS OF THE NORTH AMERICAN INDIANS, Lewis Spence. Rich anthology of the myths and legends of the Algonquins, Iroquois, Pawnees and Sioux, prefaced by an extensive historical and ethnological commentary. 36 illustrations. 480pp. 5⅜ x 8½. 25967-6 Pa. $10.95

AN ENCYCLOPEDIA OF BATTLES: Accounts of Over 1,560 Battles from 1479 B.C. to the Present, David Eggenberger. Essential details of every major battle in recorded history from the first battle of Megiddo in 1479 B.C. to Grenada in 1984. List of Battle Maps. New Appendix covering the years 1967-1984. Index. 99 illustrations. 544pp. 6½ x 9¼. 24913-1 Pa. $16.95

SAILING ALONE AROUND THE WORLD, Captain Joshua Slocum. First man to sail around the world, alone, in small boat. One of great feats of seamanship told in delightful manner. 67 illustrations. 294pp. 5⅜ x 8½. 20326-3 Pa. $6.95

ANARCHISM AND OTHER ESSAYS, Emma Goldman. Powerful, penetrating, prophetic essays on direct action, role of minorities, prison reform, puritan hypocrisy, violence, etc. 271pp. 5⅜ x 8½. 22484-8 Pa. $8.95

MYTHS OF THE HINDUS AND BUDDHISTS, Ananda K. Coomaraswamy and Sister Nivedita. Great stories of the epics; deeds of Krishna, Shiva, taken from puranas, Vedas, folk tales; etc. 32 illustrations. 400pp. 5⅜ x 8½. 21759-0 Pa. $12.95

THE TRAUMA OF BIRTH, Otto Rank. Rank's controversial thesis that anxiety neurosis is caused by profound psychological trauma which occurs at birth. 256pp. 5⅜ x 8½. 27974-X Pa. $7.95

A THEOLOGICO-POLITICAL TREATISE, Benedict Spinoza. Also contains unfinished Political Treatise. Great classic on religious liberty, theory of government on common consent. R. Elwes translation. Total of 421pp. 5⅜ x 8½. 20249-6 Pa. $10.95

MY BONDAGE AND MY FREEDOM, Frederick Douglass. Born a slave, Douglass became outspoken force in antislavery movement. The best of Douglass' autobiographies. Graphic description of slave life. 464pp. 5⅜ x 8½. 22457-0 Pa. $8.95

FOLLOWING THE EQUATOR: A Journey Around the World, Mark Twain. Fascinating humorous account of 1897 voyage to Hawaii, Australia, India, New Zealand, etc. Ironic, bemused reports on peoples, customs, climate, flora and fauna, politics, much more. 197 illustrations. 720pp. 5⅜ x 8½. 26113-1 Pa. $15.95

THE PEOPLE CALLED SHAKERS, Edward D. Andrews. Definitive study of Shakers: origins, beliefs, practices, dances, social organization, furniture and crafts, etc. 33 illustrations. 351pp. 5⅜ x 8½. 21081-2 Pa. $12.95

THE MYTHS OF GREECE AND ROME, H. A. Guerber. A classic of mythology, generously illustrated, long prized for its simple, graphic, accurate retelling of the principal myths of Greece and Rome, and for its commentary on their origins and significance. With 64 illustrations by Michelangelo, Raphael, Titian, Rubens, Canova, Bernini and others. 480pp. 5⅜ x 8½. 27584-1 Pa. $10.95

PSYCHOLOGY OF MUSIC, Carl E. Seashore. Classic work discusses music as a medium from psychological viewpoint. Clear treatment of physical acoustics, auditory apparatus, sound perception, development of musical skills, nature of musical feeling, host of other topics. 88 figures. 408pp. 5⅜ x 8½. 21851-1 Pa. $11.95

THE PHILOSOPHY OF HISTORY, Georg W. Hegel. Great classic of Western thought develops concept that history is not chance but rational process, the evolution of freedom. 457pp. 5⅜ x 8½. 20112-0 Pa. $9.95

THE BOOK OF TEA, Kakuzo Okakura. Minor classic of the Orient: entertaining, charming explanation, interpretation of traditional Japanese culture in terms of tea ceremony. 94pp. 5⅜ x 8½. 20070-1 Pa. $3.95

LIFE IN ANCIENT EGYPT, Adolf Erman. Fullest, most thorough, detailed older account with much not in more recent books, domestic life, religion, magic, medicine, commerce, much more. Many illustrations reproduce tomb paintings, carvings, hieroglyphs, etc. 597pp. 5⅜ x 8½. 22632-8 Pa. $12.95

SUNDIALS, Their Theory and Construction, Albert Waugh. Far and away the best, most thorough coverage of ideas, mathematics concerned, types, construction, adjusting anywhere. Simple, nontechnical treatment allows even children to build several of these dials. Over 100 illustrations. 230pp. 5⅜ x 8½. 22947-5 Pa. $8.95

THEORETICAL HYDRODYNAMICS, L. M. Milne-Thomson. Classic exposition of the mathematical theory of fluid motion, applicable to both hydrodynamics and aerodynamics. Over 600 exercises. 768pp. 6⅛ x 9¼. 68970-0 Pa. $20.95

SONGS OF EXPERIENCE: Facsimile Reproduction with 26 Plates in Full Color, William Blake. 26 full-color plates from a rare 1826 edition. Includes "TheTyger," "London," "Holy Thursday," and other poems. Printed text of poems. 48pp. 5¼ x 7. 24636-1 Pa. $4.95

OLD-TIME VIGNETTES IN FULL COLOR, Carol Belanger Grafton (ed.). Over 390 charming, often sentimental illustrations, selected from archives of Victorian graphics—pretty women posing, children playing, food, flowers, kittens and puppies, smiling cherubs, birds and butterflies, much more. All copyright-free. 48pp. 9¼ x 12¼. 27269-9 Pa. $9.95

PERSPECTIVE FOR ARTISTS, Rex Vicat Cole. Depth, perspective of sky and sea, shadows, much more, not usually covered. 391 diagrams, 81 reproductions of drawings and paintings. 279pp. 5⅜ x 8½. 22487-2 Pa. $9.95

DRAWING THE LIVING FIGURE, Joseph Sheppard. Innovative approach to artistic anatomy focuses on specifics of surface anatomy, rather than muscles and bones. Over 170 drawings of live models in front, back and side views, and in widely varying poses. Accompanying diagrams. 177 illustrations. Introduction. Index. 144pp. 8⅜ x11¼. 26723-7 Pa. $9.95

GOTHIC AND OLD ENGLISH ALPHABETS: 100 Complete Fonts, Dan X. Solo. Add power, elegance to posters, signs, other graphics with 100 stunning copyright-free alphabets: Blackstone, Dolbey, Germania, 97 more–including many lower-case, numerals, punctuation marks. 104pp. 8⅛ x 11. 24695-7 Pa. $9.95

HOW TO DO BEADWORK, Mary White. Fundamental book on craft from simple projects to five-bead chains and woven works. 106 illustrations. 142pp. 5⅜ x 8. 20697-1 Pa. $5.95

THE BOOK OF WOOD CARVING, Charles Marshall Sayers. Finest book for beginners discusses fundamentals and offers 34 designs. "Absolutely first rate . . . well thought out and well executed."–E. J. Tangerman. 118pp. 7¾ x 10⅝. 23654-4 Pa. $7.95

ILLUSTRATED CATALOG OF CIVIL WAR MILITARY GOODS: Union Army Weapons, Insignia, Uniform Accessories, and Other Equipment, Schuyler, Hartley, and Graham. Rare, profusely illustrated 1846 catalog includes Union Army uniform and dress regulations, arms and ammunition, coats, insignia, flags, swords, rifles, etc. 226 illustrations. 160pp. 9 x 12. 24939-5 Pa. $12.95

WOMEN'S FASHIONS OF THE EARLY 1900s: An Unabridged Republication of "New York Fashions, 1909," National Cloak & Suit Co. Rare catalog of mail-order fashions documents women's and children's clothing styles shortly after the turn of the century. Captions offer full descriptions, prices. Invaluable resource for fashion, costume historians. Approximately 725 illustrations. 128pp. 8⅜ x 11¼. 27276-1 Pa. $12.95

THE 1912 AND 1915 GUSTAV STICKLEY FURNITURE CATALOGS, Gustav Stickley. With over 200 detailed illustrations and descriptions, these two catalogs are essential reading and reference materials and identification guides for Stickley furniture. Captions cite materials, dimensions and prices. 112pp. 6½ x 9¼. 26676-1 Pa. $9.95

EARLY AMERICAN LOCOMOTIVES, John H. White, Jr. Finest locomotive engravings from early 19th century: historical (1804–74), main-line (after 1870), special, foreign, etc. 147 plates. 142pp. 11⅜ x 8¼. 22772-3 Pa. $12.95

THE TALL SHIPS OF TODAY IN PHOTOGRAPHS, Frank O. Braynard. Lavishly illustrated tribute to nearly 100 majestic contemporary sailing vessels: Amerigo Vespucci, Clearwater, Constitution, Eagle, Mayflower, Sea Cloud, Victory, many more. Authoritative captions provide statistics, background on each ship. 190 black-and-white photographs and illustrations. Introduction. 128pp. 8⅞ x 11¾. 27163-3 Pa. $14.95

LITTLE BOOK OF EARLY AMERICAN CRAFTS AND TRADES, Peter Stockham (ed.). 1807 children's book explains crafts and trades: baker, hatter, cooper, potter, and many others. 23 copperplate illustrations. 140pp. $4\frac{5}{8}$ x 6.
23336-7 Pa. $4.95

VICTORIAN FASHIONS AND COSTUMES FROM HARPER'S BAZAR, 1867–1898, Stella Blum (ed.). Day costumes, evening wear, sports clothes, shoes, hats, other accessories in over 1,000 detailed engravings. 320pp. $9\frac{3}{8}$ x $12\frac{1}{4}$.
22990-4 Pa. $16.95

GUSTAV STICKLEY, THE CRAFTSMAN, Mary Ann Smith. Superb study surveys broad scope of Stickley's achievement, especially in architecture. Design philosophy, rise and fall of the Craftsman empire, descriptions and floor plans for many Craftsman houses, more. 86 black-and-white halftones. 31 line illustrations. Introduction 208pp. $6\frac{1}{2}$ x $9\frac{1}{4}$. 27210-9 Pa. $9.95

THE LONG ISLAND RAIL ROAD IN EARLY PHOTOGRAPHS, Ron Ziel. Over 220 rare photos, informative text document origin (1844) and development of rail service on Long Island. Vintage views of early trains, locomotives, stations, passengers, crews, much more. Captions. $8\frac{7}{8}$ x $11\frac{3}{4}$. 26301-0 Pa. $14.95

VOYAGE OF THE LIBERDADE, Joshua Slocum. Great 19th-century mariner's thrilling, first-hand account of the wreck of his ship off South America, the 35-foot boat he built from the wreckage, and its remarkable voyage home. 128pp. $5\frac{3}{8}$ x $8\frac{1}{2}$.
40022-0 Pa. $5.95

TEN BOOKS ON ARCHITECTURE, Vitruvius. The most important book ever written on architecture. Early Roman aesthetics, technology, classical orders, site selection, all other aspects. Morgan translation. 331pp. $5\frac{3}{8}$ x $8\frac{1}{2}$. 20645-9 Pa. $9.95

THE HUMAN FIGURE IN MOTION, Eadweard Muybridge. More than 4,500 stopped-action photos, in action series, showing undraped men, women, children jumping, lying down, throwing, sitting, wrestling, carrying, etc. 390pp. $7\frac{7}{8}$ x $10\frac{5}{8}$.
20204-6 Clothbd. $29.95

TREES OF THE EASTERN AND CENTRAL UNITED STATES AND CANADA, William M. Harlow. Best one-volume guide to 140 trees. Full descriptions, woodlore, range, etc. Over 600 illustrations. Handy size. 288pp. $4\frac{1}{2}$ x $6\frac{3}{8}$.
20395-6 Pa. $6.95

SONGS OF WESTERN BIRDS, Dr. Donald J. Borror. Complete song and call repertoire of 60 western species, including flycatchers, juncoes, cactus wrens, many more–includes fully illustrated booklet. Cassette and manual 99913-0 $8.95

GROWING AND USING HERBS AND SPICES, Milo Miloradovich. Versatile handbook provides all the information needed for cultivation and use of all the herbs and spices available in North America. 4 illustrations. Index. Glossary. 236pp. $5\frac{3}{8}$ x $8\frac{1}{2}$.
25058-X Pa. $7.95

BIG BOOK OF MAZES AND LABYRINTHS, Walter Shepherd. 50 mazes and labyrinths in all–classical, solid, ripple, and more–in one great volume. Perfect inexpensive puzzler for clever youngsters. Full solutions. 112pp. $8\frac{1}{8}$ x 11.
22951-3 Pa. $5.95

PIANO TUNING, J. Cree Fischer. Clearest, best book for beginner, amateur. Simple repairs, raising dropped notes, tuning by easy method of flattened fifths. No previous skills needed. 4 illustrations. 201pp. 5⅜ x 8½. 23267-0 Pa. $6.95

HINTS TO SINGERS, Lillian Nordica. Selecting the right teacher, developing confidence, overcoming stage fright, and many other important skills receive thoughtful discussion in this indispensible guide, written by a world-famous diva of four decades' experience. 96pp. 5³/₈ x 8¹/₂. 40094-8 Pa. $4.95

THE COMPLETE NONSENSE OF EDWARD LEAR, Edward Lear. All nonsense limericks, zany alphabets, Owl and Pussycat, songs, nonsense botany, etc., illustrated by Lear. Total of 320pp. 5⅜ x 8½. (Available in U.S. only.) 20167-8 Pa. $7.95

VICTORIAN PARLOUR POETRY: An Annotated Anthology, Michael R. Turner. 117 gems by Longfellow, Tennyson, Browning, many lesser-known poets. "The Village Blacksmith," "Curfew Must Not Ring Tonight," "Only a Baby Small," dozens more, often difficult to find elsewhere. Index of poets, titles, first lines. xxiii + 325pp. 5⅝ x 8¼. 27044-0 Pa. $12.95

DUBLINERS, James Joyce. Fifteen stories offer vivid, tightly focused observations of the lives of Dublin's poorer classes. At least one, "The Dead," is considered a masterpiece. Reprinted complete and unabridged from standard edition. 160pp. 5³⁄₁₆ x 8¼. 26870-5 Pa. $1.50

GREAT WEIRD TALES: 14 Stories by Lovecraft, Blackwood, Machen and Others, S. T. Joshi (ed.). 14 spellbinding tales, including "The Sin Eater," by Fiona McLeod, "The Eye Above the Mantel," by Frank Belknap Long, as well as renowned works by R. H. Barlow, Lord Dunsany, Arthur Machen, W. C. Morrow and eight other masters of the genre. 256pp. 5⅜ x 8½. (Available in U.S. only.) 40436-6 Pa. $8.95

THE BOOK OF THE SACRED MAGIC OF ABRAMELIN THE MAGE, translated by S. MacGregor Mathers. Medieval manuscript of ceremonial magic. Basic document in Aleister Crowley, Golden Dawn groups. 268pp. 5⅜ x 8½. 23211-5 Pa. $9.95

NEW RUSSIAN-ENGLISH AND ENGLISH-RUSSIAN DICTIONARY, M. A. O'Brien. This is a remarkably handy Russian dictionary, containing a surprising amount of information, including over 70,000 entries. 366pp. 4½ x 6⅛. 20208-9 Pa. $10.95

HISTORIC HOMES OF THE AMERICAN PRESIDENTS, Second, Revised Edition, Irvin Haas. A traveler's guide to American Presidential homes, most open to the public, depicting and describing homes occupied by every American President from George Washington to George Bush. With visiting hours, admission charges, travel routes. 175 photographs. Index. 160pp. 8¼ x 11. 26751-2 Pa. $13.95

NEW YORK IN THE FORTIES, Andreas Feininger. 162 brilliant photographs by the well-known photographer, formerly with *Life* magazine. Commuters, shoppers, Times Square at night, much else from city at its peak. Captions by John von Hartz. 181pp. 9¼ x 10¾. 23585-8 Pa. $13.95

INDIAN SIGN LANGUAGE, William Tomkins. Over 525 signs developed by Sioux and other tribes. Written instructions and diagrams. Also 290 pictographs. 111pp. 6⅛ x 9¼. 22029-X Pa. $3.95

ANATOMY: A Complete Guide for Artists, Joseph Sheppard. A master of figure drawing shows artists how to render human anatomy convincingly. Over 460 illustrations. 224pp. 8⅜ x 11¼. 27279-6 Pa. $11.95

MEDIEVAL CALLIGRAPHY: Its History and Technique, Marc Drogin. Spirited history, comprehensive instruction manual covers 13 styles (ca. 4th century through 15th). Excellent photographs; directions for duplicating medieval techniques with modern tools. 224pp. 8⅜ x 11¼. 26142-5 Pa. $12.95

DRIED FLOWERS: How to Prepare Them, Sarah Whitlock and Martha Rankin. Complete instructions on how to use silica gel, meal and borax, perlite aggregate, sand and borax, glycerine and water to create attractive permanent flower arrangements. 12 illustrations. 32pp. 5⅜ x 8½. 21802-3 Pa. $1.00

EASY-TO-MAKE BIRD FEEDERS FOR WOODWORKERS, Scott D. Campbell. Detailed, simple-to-use guide for designing, constructing, caring for and using feeders. Text, illustrations for 12 classic and contemporary designs. 96pp. 5⅜ x 8½. 25847-5 Pa. $3.95

SCOTTISH WONDER TALES FROM MYTH AND LEGEND, Donald A. Mackenzie. 16 lively tales tell of giants rumbling down mountainsides, of a magic wand that turns stone pillars into warriors, of gods and goddesses, evil hags, powerful forces and more. 240pp. 5⅜ x 8½. 29677-6 Pa. $6.95

THE HISTORY OF UNDERCLOTHES, C. Willett Cunnington and Phyllis Cunnington. Fascinating, well-documented survey covering six centuries of English undergarments, enhanced with over 100 illustrations: 12th-century laced-up bodice, footed long drawers (1795), 19th-century bustles, 19th-century corsets for men, Victorian "bust improvers," much more. 272pp. 5⅝ x 8¼. 27124-2 Pa. $9.95

ARTS AND CRAFTS FURNITURE: The Complete Brooks Catalog of 1912, Brooks Manufacturing Co. Photos and detailed descriptions of more than 150 now very collectible furniture designs from the Arts and Crafts movement depict davenports, settees, buffets, desks, tables, chairs, bedsteads, dressers and more, all built of solid, quarter-sawed oak. Invaluable for students and enthusiasts of antiques, Americana and the decorative arts. 80pp. 6½ x 9¼. 27471-3 Pa. $8.95

WILBUR AND ORVILLE: A Biography of the Wright Brothers, Fred Howard. Definitive, crisply written study tells the full story of the brothers' lives and work. A vividly written biography, unparalleled in scope and color, that also captures the spirit of an extraordinary era. 560pp. 6⅛ x 9¼. 40297-5 Pa. $17.95

THE ARTS OF THE SAILOR: Knotting, Splicing and Ropework, Hervey Garrett Smith. Indispensable shipboard reference covers tools, basic knots and useful hitches; handsewing and canvas work, more. Over 100 illustrations. Delightful reading for sea lovers. 256pp. 5⅜ x 8½. 26440-8 Pa. $8.95

FRANK LLOYD WRIGHT'S FALLINGWATER: The House and Its History, Second, Revised Edition, Donald Hoffmann. A total revision–both in text and illustrations–of the standard document on Fallingwater, the boldest, most personal architectural statement of Wright's mature years, updated with valuable new material from the recently opened Frank Lloyd Wright Archives. "Fascinating"–*The New York Times*. 116 illustrations. 128pp. 9¼ x 10¾. 27430-6 Pa. $12.95

PHOTOGRAPHIC SKETCHBOOK OF THE CIVIL WAR, Alexander Gardner. 100 photos taken on field during the Civil War. Famous shots of Manassas Harper's Ferry, Lincoln, Richmond, slave pens, etc. 244pp. 10⅝ x 8¼. 22731-6 Pa. $10.95

FIVE ACRES AND INDEPENDENCE, Maurice G. Kains. Great back-to-the-land classic explains basics of self-sufficient farming. The one book to get. 95 illustrations. 397pp. 5⅜ x 8½. 20974-1 Pa. $7.95

SONGS OF EASTERN BIRDS, Dr. Donald J. Borror. Songs and calls of 60 species most common to eastern U.S.: warblers, woodpeckers, flycatchers, thrushes, larks, many more in high-quality recording. Cassette and manual 99912-2 $9.95

A MODERN HERBAL, Margaret Grieve. Much the fullest, most exact, most useful compilation of herbal material. Gigantic alphabetical encyclopedia, from aconite to zedoary, gives botanical information, medical properties, folklore, economic uses, much else. Indispensable to serious reader. 161 illustrations. 888pp. 6½ x 9¼. 2-vol. set. (Available in U.S. only.) Vol. I: 22798-7 Pa. $10.95
Vol. II: 22799-5 Pa. $10.95

HIDDEN TREASURE MAZE BOOK, Dave Phillips. Solve 34 challenging mazes accompanied by heroic tales of adventure. Evil dragons, people-eating plants, blood-thirsty giants, many more dangerous adversaries lurk at every twist and turn. 34 mazes, stories, solutions. 48pp. 8¼ x 11. 24566-7 Pa. $2.95

LETTERS OF W. A. MOZART, Wolfgang A. Mozart. Remarkable letters show bawdy wit, humor, imagination, musical insights, contemporary musical world; includes some letters from Leopold Mozart. 276pp. 5⅜ x 8½. 22859-2 Pa. $9.95

BASIC PRINCIPLES OF CLASSICAL BALLET, Agrippina Vaganova. Great Russian theoretician, teacher explains methods for teaching classical ballet. 118 illustrations. 175pp. 5⅜ x 8½. 22036-2 Pa. $6.95

THE JUMPING FROG, Mark Twain. Revenge edition. The original story of The Celebrated Jumping Frog of Calaveras County, a hapless French translation, and Twain's hilarious "retranslation" from the French. 12 illustrations. 66pp. 5⅜ x 8½. 22686-7 Pa. $4.95

BEST REMEMBERED POEMS, Martin Gardner (ed.). The 126 poems in this superb collection of 19th- and 20th-century British and American verse range from Shelley's "To a Skylark" to the impassioned "Renascence" of Edna St. Vincent Millay and to Edward Lear's whimsical "The Owl and the Pussycat." 224pp. 5⅜ x 8½. 27165-X Pa. $5.95

COMPLETE SONNETS, William Shakespeare. Over 150 exquisite poems deal with love, friendship, the tyranny of time, beauty's evanescence, death and other themes in language of remarkable power, precision and beauty. Glossary of archaic terms. 80pp. 5³⁄₁₆ x 8¼. 26686-9 Pa. $1.00

THE BATTLES THAT CHANGED HISTORY, Fletcher Pratt. Eminent historian profiles 16 crucial conflicts, ancient to modern, that changed the course of civilization. 352pp. 5⅜ x 8½. 41129-X Pa. $9.95

THE WIT AND HUMOR OF OSCAR WILDE, Alvin Redman (ed.). More than 1,000 ripostes, paradoxes, wisecracks: Work is the curse of the drinking classes; I can resist everything except temptation; etc. 258pp. 5⅜ x 8½.   20602-5 Pa. $6.95

SHAKESPEARE LEXICON AND QUOTATION DICTIONARY, Alexander Schmidt. Full definitions, locations, shades of meaning in every word in plays and poems. More than 50,000 exact quotations. 1,485pp. 6½ x 9¼. 2-vol. set.

Vol. 1: 22726-X Pa. $17.95
Vol. 2: 22727-8 Pa. $17.95

SELECTED POEMS, Emily Dickinson. Over 100 best-known, best-loved poems by one of America's foremost poets, reprinted from authoritative early editions. No comparable edition at this price. Index of first lines. 64pp. 5³⁄₁₆ x 8¼.

26466-1 Pa. $1.00

THE INSIDIOUS DR. FU-MANCHU, Sax Rohmer. The first of the popular mystery series introduces a pair of English detectives to their archnemesis, the diabolical Dr. Fu-Manchu. Flavorful atmosphere, fast-paced action, and colorful characters enliven this classic of the genre. 208pp. 5³⁄₁₆ x 8¼.   29898-1 Pa. $2.00

THE MALLEUS MALEFICARUM OF KRAMER AND SPRENGER, translated by Montague Summers. Full text of most important witchhunter's "bible," used by both Catholics and Protestants. 278pp. 6⅝ x 10.   22802-9 Pa. $12.95

SPANISH STORIES/CUENTOS ESPAÑOLES: A Dual-Language Book, Angel Flores (ed.). Unique format offers 13 great stories in Spanish by Cervantes, Borges, others. Faithful English translations on facing pages. 352pp. 5⅜ x 8½.

25399-6 Pa. $9.95

GARDEN CITY, LONG ISLAND, IN EARLY PHOTOGRAPHS, 1869–1919, Mildred H. Smith. Handsome treasury of 118 vintage pictures, accompanied by carefully researched captions, document the Garden City Hotel fire (1899), the Vanderbilt Cup Race (1908), the first airmail flight departing from the Nassau Boulevard Aerodrome (1911), and much more. 96pp. 8⅞ x 11³⁄₄.   40669-5 Pa. $12.95

OLD QUEENS, N.Y., IN EARLY PHOTOGRAPHS, Vincent F. Seyfried and William Asadorian. Over 160 rare photographs of Maspeth, Jamaica, Jackson Heights, and other areas. Vintage views of DeWitt Clinton mansion, 1939 World's Fair and more. Captions. 192pp. 8⅞ x 11.   26358-4 Pa. $14.95

CAPTURED BY THE INDIANS: 15 Firsthand Accounts, 1750-1870, Frederick Drimmer. Astounding true historical accounts of grisly torture, bloody conflicts, relentless pursuits, miraculous escapes and more, by people who lived to tell the tale. 384pp. 5⅜ x 8½.   24901-8 Pa. $9.95

THE WORLD'S GREAT SPEECHES (Fourth Enlarged Edition), Lewis Copeland, Lawrence W. Lamm, and Stephen J. McKenna. Nearly 300 speeches provide public speakers with a wealth of updated quotes and inspiration–from Pericles' funeral oration and William Jennings Bryan's "Cross of Gold Speech" to Malcolm X's powerful words on the Black Revolution and Earl of Spenser's tribute to his sister, Diana, Princess of Wales. 944pp. 5⅜ x 8⅜.   40903-1 Pa. $15.95

THE BOOK OF THE SWORD, Sir Richard F. Burton. Great Victorian scholar/adventurer's eloquent, erudite history of the "queen of weapons"–from prehistory to early Roman Empire. Evolution and development of early swords, variations (sabre, broadsword, cutlass, scimitar, etc.), much more. 336pp. 6⅛ x 9¼.

25434-8 Pa. $9.95

AUTOBIOGRAPHY: The Story of My Experiments with Truth, Mohandas K. Gandhi. Boyhood, legal studies, purification, the growth of the Satyagraha (nonviolent protest) movement. Critical, inspiring work of the man responsible for the freedom of India. 480pp. 5⅜ x 8½. (Available in U.S. only.) 24593-4 Pa. $9.95

CELTIC MYTHS AND LEGENDS, T. W. Rolleston. Masterful retelling of Irish and Welsh stories and tales. Cuchulain, King Arthur, Deirdre, the Grail, many more. First paperback edition. 58 full-page illustrations. 512pp. 5⅜ x 8½. 26507-2 Pa. $9.95

THE PRINCIPLES OF PSYCHOLOGY, William James. Famous long course complete, unabridged. Stream of thought, time perception, memory, experimental methods; great work decades ahead of its time. 94 figures. 1,391pp. 5⅜ x 8½. 2-vol. set.
Vol. I: 20381-6 Pa. $14.95
Vol. II: 20382-4 Pa. $16.95

THE WORLD AS WILL AND REPRESENTATION, Arthur Schopenhauer. Definitive English translation of Schopenhauer's life work, correcting more than 1,000 errors, omissions in earlier translations. Translated by E. F. J. Payne. Total of 1,269pp. 5⅜ x 8½. 2-vol. set. Vol. 1: 21761-2 Pa. $12.95
Vol. 2: 21762-0 Pa. $12.95

MAGIC AND MYSTERY IN TIBET, Madame Alexandra David-Neel. Experiences among lamas, magicians, sages, sorcerers, Bonpa wizards. A true psychic discovery. 32 illustrations. 321pp. 5⅜ x 8½. (Available in U.S. only.) 22682-4 Pa. $9.95

THE EGYPTIAN BOOK OF THE DEAD, E. A. Wallis Budge. Complete reproduction of Ani's papyrus, finest ever found. Full hieroglyphic text, interlinear transliteration, word-for-word translation, smooth translation. 533pp. 6½ x 9¼.
21866-X Pa. $12.95

MATHEMATICS FOR THE NONMATHEMATICIAN, Morris Kline. Detailed, college-level treatment of mathematics in cultural and historical context, with numerous exercises. Recommended Reading Lists. Tables. Numerous figures. 641pp. 5⅜ x 8½.
24823-2 Pa. $11.95

PROBABILISTIC METHODS IN THE THEORY OF STRUCTURES, Isaac Elishakoff. Well-written introduction covers the elements of the theory of probability from two or more random variables, the reliability of such multivariable structures, the theory of random function, Monte Carlo methods of treating problems incapable of exact solution, and more. Examples. 502pp. 5³/₈ x 8¹/₂. 40691-1 Pa. $16.95

THE RIME OF THE ANCIENT MARINER, Gustave Doré, S. T. Coleridge. Doré's finest work; 34 plates capture moods, subtleties of poem. Flawless full-size reproductions printed on facing pages with authoritative text of poem. "Beautiful. Simply beautiful."–*Publisher's Weekly*. 77pp. 9¼ x 12. 22305-1 Pa. $7.95

NORTH AMERICAN INDIAN DESIGNS FOR ARTISTS AND CRAFTSPEOPLE, Eva Wilson. Over 360 authentic copyright-free designs adapted from Navajo blankets, Hopi pottery, Sioux buffalo hides, more. Geometrics, symbolic figures, plant and animal motifs, etc. 128pp. 8⅜ x 11. (Not for sale in the United Kingdom.) 25341-4 Pa. $9.95

SCULPTURE: Principles and Practice, Louis Slobodkin. Step-by-step approach to clay, plaster, metals, stone; classical and modern. 253 drawings, photos. 255pp. 8⅛ x 11.
22960-2 Pa. $11.95

THE INFLUENCE OF SEA POWER UPON HISTORY, 1660–1783, A. T. Mahan. Influential classic of naval history and tactics still used as text in war colleges. First paperback edition. 4 maps. 24 battle plans. 640pp. 5⅜ x 8½.   25509-3 Pa. $14.95

THE STORY OF THE TITANIC AS TOLD BY ITS SURVIVORS, Jack Winocour (ed.). What it was really like. Panic, despair, shocking inefficiency, and a little heroism. More thrilling than any fictional account. 26 illustrations. 320pp. 5⅜ x 8½.
20610-6 Pa. $8.95

FAIRY AND FOLK TALES OF THE IRISH PEASANTRY, William Butler Yeats (ed.). Treasury of 64 tales from the twilight world of Celtic myth and legend: "The Soul Cages," "The Kildare Pooka," "King O'Toole and his Goose," many more. Introduction and Notes by W. B. Yeats. 352pp. 5⅜ x 8½.   26941-8 Pa. $8.95

BUDDHIST MAHAYANA TEXTS, E. B. Cowell and others (eds.). Superb, accurate translations of basic documents in Mahayana Buddhism, highly important in history of religions. The Buddha-karita of Asvaghosha, Larger Sukhavativyuha, more. 448pp. 5⅜ x 8½.   25552-2 Pa. $12.95

ONE TWO THREE . . . INFINITY: Facts and Speculations of Science, George Gamow. Great physicist's fascinating, readable overview of contemporary science: number theory, relativity, fourth dimension, entropy, genes, atomic structure, much more. 128 illustrations. Index. 352pp. 5⅜ x 8½.   25664-2 Pa. $9.95

EXPERIMENTATION AND MEASUREMENT, W. J. Youden. Introductory manual explains laws of measurement in simple terms and offers tips for achieving accuracy and minimizing errors. Mathematics of measurement, use of instruments, experimenting with machines. 1994 edition. Foreword. Preface. Introduction. Epilogue. Selected Readings. Glossary. Index. Tables and figures. 128pp. 5³/₈ x 8¹/₂.
40451-X Pa. $6.95

DALÍ ON MODERN ART: The Cuckolds of Antiquated Modern Art, Salvador Dalí. Influential painter skewers modern art and its practitioners. Outrageous evaluations of Picasso, Cézanne, Turner, more. 15 renderings of paintings discussed. 44 calligraphic decorations by Dalí. 96pp. 5⅜ x 8½. (Available in U.S. only.)   29220-7 Pa. $5.95

ANTIQUE PLAYING CARDS: A Pictorial History, Henry René D'Allemagne. Over 900 elaborate, decorative images from rare playing cards (14th–20th centuries): Bacchus, death, dancing dogs, hunting scenes, royal coats of arms, players cheating, much more. 96pp. 9¼ x 12¼.   29265-7 Pa. $12.95

MAKING FURNITURE MASTERPIECES: 30 Projects with Measured Drawings, Franklin H. Gottshall. Step-by-step instructions, illustrations for constructing handsome, useful pieces, among them a Sheraton desk, Chippendale chair, Spanish desk, Queen Anne table and a William and Mary dressing mirror. 224pp. 8⅛ x 11¼.
29338-6 Pa. $16.95

THE FOSSIL BOOK: A Record of Prehistoric Life, Patricia V. Rich et al. Profusely illustrated definitive guide covers everything from single-celled organisms and dinosaurs to birds and mammals and the interplay between climate and man. Over 1,500 illustrations. 760pp. 7½ x 10⅛.   29371-8 Pa. $29.95

Prices subject to change without notice.